Crisis of
Conscience

Crisis of Conscience

Arkansas Methodists and the Civil Rights Struggle

Butler Center for Arkansas Studies
Central Arkansas Library System

Edited by
James T. Clemons
and Kelly L. Farr

The Butler Center for Arkansas Studies
Central Arkansas Library System
100 Rock Street
Little Rock, Arkansas 72201

ISBN: 978-0-9708574-4-6

Library of Congress Cataloging-in-Publication Data

Crisis of conscience : Arkansas Methodism and the civil rights crisis /
James T. Clemons and Kelly L. Farr, editors.
    p. cm.
  Includes bibliographical references.
  ISBN-13: 978-0-9708574-4-6 (pbk.)
  1. African Americans--Civil rights--Arkansas--History--20th century. 2.
African Americans--Segregation--Arkansas--History--20th century. 3. Civil
rights movements--Arkansas--History--20th century. 4.
Methodists--Arkansas--Political activity--History--20th century. 5.
Whites--Arkansas--Biography. 6. Methodists--Arkansas--Biography. 7.
Methodist Church--Arkansas--History--20th century. 8. Civil
rights--Religious aspects--Christianity--History--20th century. 9.
Arkansas--Race relations--History--20th century. 10. Arkansas--Church
history. I. Clemons, James T. II. Farr, Kelly L., 1970-
  E185.93.A8C75 2007
  323.0973--dc22
                                    2007014559

The Butler Center for Arkansas Studies, a department of the Central Arkansas
Library System, was created in 1997 through an endowment by the late Richard
C. Butler, Sr., of Little Rock, for the purpose of promoting a greater understanding and appreciation of Arkansas history, literature, art, and culture. For more
information, please call 501.918.3049 or visit www.butlercenter.org.

Printed in the United States of America.

Table of Contents

Foreword

Long before Governor Orval Faubus used his executive authority to order the Arkansas National Guard to prevent integration at Little Rock Central High School in 1957, and President Dwight D. Eisenhower used his authority as Commander-in-Chief to nationalize those Arkansas guardsmen, whites and blacks were meeting together.

Long before the Supreme Court's decision in *Brown v. Board of Education* in 1954, blacks and whites were seeking to break down the walls of racial segregation.

And long before the struggle for civil rights became The Movement in America, people in Arkansas were, as best they could, promoting harmony and equality, peace and justice among the races. Many of those Arkansans were Methodists.

Some of them were at the epicenter of the crisis and in the national media spotlight. Others were never mentioned, even in a local newspaper, and were unknown except to family, close friends and neighbors. Their stories are poignant, telling of courage and suffering, faith and love. More than just accounts, however, they reveal the sordid conditions of life among blacks, their fear and horror of daily life arising from prejudice and hatred. They also reveal the soul searching reflections of individuals, and institutions, on what they did and did not do, ending with a profound analysis of their crisis of conscience.

For several years, I kept waiting for someone to collect and publish accounts of close friends I knew who had worked hard, stood bravely and were punished for their Christian witness during the Civil Rights movement. Time passed too quickly. So many will recall and give thanks with me for the lives and memories of Ferris Baker, Jim Beal, Lamar Davis, Vernon Paysinger and Bill Wilder. I began to fear that the stories of others might never be told. One day, I jotted down on a small, spiral notepad the title for this book.

It is written, then, by default. I wish someone else, far better qualified, had undertaken it. From biblical times to the present, people have responded to a call by asking, "Who, me?" I am just one more in a long line of "Who me's."

Even so, the book appears now, almost fifty years after that fateful moment in history on the steps of Little Rock Central High School. It is published with the fervent hope that its stories will bring enlightenment on a significant era and inspiration to present and future Methodists, and others, in Arkansas and beyond.

The personal stories, as well as the histories of Camp Aldersgate, Hendrix College and Philander Smith College, with few exceptions, have never been told. They now become part of the recorded history of Methodism, Arkansas and America.

Jim Clemons
October 17, 2006

Acknowledgements

It is with an enormous sense of gratitude that I list the names of those who have in so many ways given loving support in making possible this book. Heading that list is Kelly Farr, a superb coeditor in every way. She scrutinized each contribution, made revisions on which we conferred, made the final changes and typed the entire manuscript to be camera ready for publication. She made exceptional use of her graduate certificate in scholarly publishing from Arizona State University and her experience in editing with a major denominational publishing house. Through it all she maintained an encouraging optimism and enthusiasm for the project and was ever a joy to work with through our long hours on the phone.

David Stricklin, Department Head of the Butler Center for Arkansas Studies in the Central Arkansas Library System, gave his generous backing and offered advice at several points, as did his colleague Holly Mathisen. Holly managed all of my requests for information and guidance. They never expressed questions as to the worthiness of what we were about.

For any team effort to succeed there has to be a strong support system. Craig and Nancy Wood were there for us from the beginning, long before we had a publisher and with only a few stories in hand. With her own background in journalism, including editorship of *The Arkansas Traveler* at the University of Arkansas in Fayetteville, Nancy also gave a bit of needed editorial help.

Each of the contributors drew upon memories, often painful to recall, or did extensive research. Some close friends agreed to my initial personal request, others responded to the Arkansas Conference email appeal for stories, and a few were approached after their names had been suggested to me. Reading their accounts, some several times, was always rewarding. Taken together, they were an inspiration.

Crisis of Conscience is a phrase taken from John Workman's story. It proved to be a most fitting title for the book.

Each of those whose names are listed below will know why they are mentioned, but never the extent of my thanks.

Lou Angelo
Joan Baker
Mauzel Beal
Ray Bruce
Roger K. Bryles
Margaret E. Clemons
Marcia Cox
Jane Dennis
Pam Dyson
David and Billile Hill
Jajuan Johnson

Marie Jordan
Walter N. Kimbrough
Jim Lane
Freddie and Vic Nixon
Grace Ellen Rice
Grif Stockley
Sheila Vancura
Eleanor Vander Haegen
    and Susan Sielke
Sarah Wacaster
Gene and Meredith Wilbourn

A Word about Methodism

Throughout the stories and articles that follow, references are made to different Methodist denominations. This brief overview might be helpful to those readers unfamiliar with Methodist history and polity.

The founder of Methodism was John Wesley, 1709-1803, an Anglican minister, university scholar, theologian, prolific writer and indefatigable preacher in England, Ireland and Wales. For a time, he was in America with General Oglethorpe in Georgia.

Upon his return to England, he resumed his teaching at Oxford University. The term Methodist was used at Oxford where John Wesley, his brother Charles, and others in that academic community followed a rigid pattern of prayer, exercise and community service, especially in prisons, and attending to the many needs of the poor and uneducated. Someone referred to them derisively as "methodists," for their methodical ways, which Wesley took as a badge of honor.

Wesley became much concerned that the established church was not reaching many of the common folk, especially poor farmers, industrial workers, and prisoners. His response was to organize societies, find and train preachers, appoint them to ride circuits, and meet with them once a year. These "annual conferences" continue to this day, and the term also refers to specific geographical areas. Often such conferences are combined, as were the White River, North Arkansas and Little Rock Conferences, which are now the Arkansas Conference. Each conference is presided over by a bishop.

Gradually, Methodists turned up in different parts of America and the movement quickly grew. But the "preachers" were not ordained and so not permitted to administer the sacraments, which was reserved for ordained clergy, some of whom were supportive of the new growing number of Methodists. With the onset of the American Revolution, the English colonists were often suspected and mistreated because of their strong ties to England. Many of the Anglican ministers returned home. John Wesley reluctantly agreed to allow the organization of a Methodist Church in America, but not in England. The first annual conference for the new Methodist Episcopal Church was held in Baltimore in 1774, patterned after its parent church.

Although extremely well organized, the movement was always within the bounds of the established church. Wesley never heeded calls for a separate denomination, and insisted that meetings of the societies were never to be held at times of regular Anglican worship services. But the American spirit of independence was strong and led to the break-away Protestant Methodist Church in the late 1770s. Its slogan was, "A church without a bishop in a country without a king."

The major division within American Methodism came prior to the Civil War over the question of whether or not a bishop could own slaves. The Methodist Episcopal Church, South (MECS) was dominant among the Confederate States. In 1939, The Methodist Episcopal Church, The Methodist Episcopal Church, South, and The Methodist Protestant Church united to form The Methodist Church. They established the Central Conference that included all black Methodist churches, regardless of their location within the United States, and had districts within that conference. In Arkansas, all black Methodist churches were in the Southwest District of the Central Conference. In 1968, The Methodist Church joined with the United Brethren Church, which had strong German roots, to become The United Methodist Church. Other branches of Methodism, such as The Free Methodist Church, were formed for different reasons.

* * *

Though this volume concentrates mostly on white Methodist churches in the South, we hope that in the future other Methodist denominations will bring forth their own accounts of events during the Civil Rights movement.

All Is Not Yet Well
Bob Bearden

I would like to begin by saying straight off, I disavow any claims of having done anything really strong, significant or courageous in this most earnest struggle of civil rights. I do feel, though, that I had some considerable influence with the people in my church, in the community, and even in the state-at-large.

My wife Ellen and I began our ministry together in the fall of 1938. For nine years we served small churches and some reasonably larger ones in the delta region of northeast Arkansas. We later moved to the western part of the state, first to Fort Smith and then to Central Methodist Church in Fayetteville, which served the University of Arkansas. That was the very beginning of my experience with integration. The people were very liberal and very alert. The public schools integrated the black and white students even before the 1954 Supreme Court order. There were very few blacks there, of course, but there was a spirit of openness. We did not encounter much trouble there because of that spirit.

A dramatic change occurred in my ministry in 1960, however. I was sent to First Methodist Church in Little Rock, after Bishop Aubrey Walton was elected to the episcopacy. It was a church downtown, founded in 1831. I served an older, conservative congregation, which had struggled through some bad times making it an unusually sensitive congregation. About three months before my arrival there in June, a state-wide Methodist meeting was held at the church. Bishop Paul A. Martin was in charge. He was handed a note saying they had received a telephone call indicating there was a bomb in the basement right under the sanctuary, and it was set to explode in just a few minutes.

Bishop Martin calmly said to those in attendance, "We have received this note saying there is a bomb in the church. We are going to sing a hymn. While we are singing, all those who would like to leave are urged to do so, and we will make no judgment on you at all." The report was that only three or four people left. The rest stayed. Nothing happened.

13

Just before I arrived in Little Rock, a few young men from Philander Smith College, founded for freedmen just after the Civil War, attended a Sunday morning service at First Methodist. The college was only six blocks from the church. After the service had begun, the news media came in with lights and took pictures. This raised a real commotion. The church leaders said, "We will no longer allow blacks to come to worship." When I came, I did not do anything bold, but I did work on the issue of attendance. And, fortunately, we were able to work it out. Things settled down a bit, but we had our problems just the same.

Later, in the same church, a young adult class, several of whose members had small children, were concerned about the church's lack of social mission. Our young associate pastor, Ed Matthews, was a leader for the group who called themselves Koinonia. They decided to start a day care center for working mothers, blacks as well as whites. Just after it began, we started receiving complaints. One of the most important members of the church, and I underscore he was one of the leaders, well established in the city, as well as the church, called me and said, "If you accept these young black children, they will want to come to Sunday school, and their families will want to come to church, and then you will be in big trouble."

I was able to give him a good and reasonable answer. "We have a large number of young adults with families in our church who are extremely restless about our lack of mission work. These are the leaders of that group, and they want to establish the day care center. 'But we will not,' they said, 'have anything to do with it if it is not integrated.' If we don't come through with this, we will see an exodus out of the church that is going to be shocking."

Needless to say, the day care center went forward; its growth was remarkable. I have never seen anything like it. It became totally accepted in and around our area. Thirty years later it is the largest in Arkansas, nearly three hundred children. One of the leading families in Little Rock made it possible to buy a large building near the church and have it remodeled so that it could have the finest facilities. It now bears the name of the woman whose family made that possible. It is a project to be proud of.

At this point, I would like to say a word to today's young ministers about the spirit of those times. You would have had to have been there to believe the volatility that the constant actions of racism were caus-ing—fear, anger, division among families, business offices, and church-es. You cannot imagine the pressure placed upon pastors. I am not try-ing to give us a saintly, angelic look. We were far from that. But it was a very bad thing, and any movement toward integration would give you a liberal reputation, meaning that no church would accept you, even the smallest churches. I do think violence was close at hand. I believe it was so sharp there could have been a minor war in the streets of the city. But I am sure the wrong we were trying to right could very well bring a minister down. Things are quite different in Little Rock and the state now, and in the United Methodist Church also, but I will not elab-orate on that now. It would seem all was right. But all is not yet well.

Through Grace
Sylvia Bell

As Methodists and as Christians, we all have our stories of faith and our relationships with Jesus Christ. I met Jesus one morning at the Old Bethlehem CME (Colored Methodist Episcopal) Church with its little parsonage. One day, Jesus was standing there beside this little five-year-old girl, me, who had answered a question about him in Sunday school. That is how my story begins. Most of us view our stories as being significant to no one but ourselves. I like to think God positioned me to tell this story even though it contains memories that hurt. It is a story of receiving God's grace. It is a story of being graced through grace. The Creator of heaven and earth is active in a continual process of creating and recreating, molding and shaping me.

In 1953, I looked across from the Bethlehem CME Church longing to enter the doors of the Julius Rosenwald African American School with my siblings. I leaned out as far as I could on the doorstep to hear the voices resonating from the school's open door. My siblings and cousins, as well as my Dad who taught there as a substitute after completing eighth grade, fed my longing to enter through the door, which surely contained wisdom.

I never attended the African American school, however, for in 1954, the Charleston public school system integrated. Before school started that year, the school's superintendent came to our home to speak with my parents. I remember one of her remarks, "Send your kids to school clean, without runny noses." I've learned over the years that that racial slur was expressed to many African American families as desegregation took place all over the South in the 1950s. My mother's response was always the same, "We always send our kids to school clean. We never send them dirty. They might wear the same clothes more than once a week, but they are clean."

I started first grade that year. I was so happy finally to be going to school. I would have books, and I would learn how to read them. As I stepped off the bus that first day, full of hope, I heard, "Hey, nigger." In my church denomination, we speak of the laying on of the hands. Well, I was about to lay hands of a different kind on him, all the while hearing my mother in the back of mind saying, "Don't start nothing, but take care of yourselves. Stand up for your rights." I was standing up for my rights, and he was within my grasp.

Then, there she was, the principal. "What do you think you're doing?" She was wearing a khaki jacket with a matching tight skirt. "He called me a nigger," I said. She replied, "Well, that's what you are!" I was stunned. I stopped in my tracks. It was a slap in the face. I turned away, defeated.

I had finally started school and had it ruined by receiving a racial slur, which is a sin. This slur was a form of demoralization of a race, and also of a little girl. The sin was perpetuated by the woman in authority. I had looked to her for affirmation. She had the power to be my liberator; however, she chose to be my abuser, oppressor, and to demoralize me further by affirming the slur, the sin. For every evil there is a good which shines forth so much brighter. I was fortunate to have a good first grade teacher that year. Regardless of what her beliefs or prejudices were, she did not show them. She was a teacher, and she helped me learn.

I so admire the students who participated in the Little Rock Central High School desegregation in 1957. Those students struggled under a spotlight of ungodly racial prejudices. But three years earlier, Charleston's schools quietly integrated with few problems. After a while, we fell into a routine of laughing, talking, and studying with friends who were brave enough not to care what others said or who were so ostracized themselves, that in spite of what their peers or parents said, it did not matter where the hospitality came from. At the end of the school year, we all went our separate ways. We worked hard, played hard, had leisure days of summer, and then were ready to return to school to see friends and class mates.

We have the power to make a real Garden of Eden. However, unrest, ignorance, prejudices, oppression, domination, and discontent seem always to filter into the most peaceful of gardens. The sticks and stones that break bones are not as dangerous as the demoralizing words that do hurt us and remain with us forever. Remarks such as "the South will rise again" still reverberate throughout the South. Phrases like, "hey, nigger" and "I can't play with you anymore because you're a nigger" still echo in my head.

This is my story, but it also becomes a thank you to everyone who has provided support to me along the way. The things we do, the care we give, and especially the powerful words of hope and encouragement that have been spoken really do make a difference in a life. A little girl stepped off the bus and heard, "Hey, nigger," and "That's what you are." It could have chosen my path for life.

I am thankful for the call to the ministry in The United Methodist Church as pastor of two all-white churches here in Arkansas. It has been a challenging and worthwhile ministry. I know for a fact that God has been with me every step of the way—graced by grace.

Editors' Note:

The Reverend Ms. Bell was appointed pastor of St. Andrews United Methodist Church in Little Rock at the June 2006 Arkansas Annual Conference.

Julius Rosenwald (1862-1932) was an American merchant and philanthropist. He established the Julius Rosenwald Fund in 1917, which has contributed more than twenty-eight million dollars to schools and facilities throughout the rural South.

Love's Injunctions
Angie Evans Benham

Driving through my childhood neighborhood in Van Buren, Arkansas, toward the old St. John's Methodist Church, I notice a dark line of chained-together auditorium seats placed under an aluminum canopy. I recognize those seats and then recall that Butterfield Junior High published an auction notice because of its recent remodeling. In my day, both junior and senior high school students utilized those seats for viewing school play productions, even a *Pirates of Penzance* operetta, assemblies that allowed traveling entertainers to show us human magic or the tricks of trained animals, and more serious matters as well. Recitals, graduations, and matters of public interest occurred in that brick auditorium. A matter of public interest took me to the auditorium on a September night in 1958, and my stand for integration of Van Buren High School that night created changes in my life that have continued for almost fifty years.

Coming back to Van Buren after my years in other states, I don't know the stranger who now owns the auditorium seats, nor the people, some brown-skinned with a different language, who live in the homes still associated in my mind with members of St. John's. Originally called "Long Bell" and then East Van Buren Methodist Episcopal Church, South, St. John's fusion with First Methodist produced Heritage United Methodist Church, a large congregation filled with newcomers my mother envisioned when she said "they will want something better for their children than we have." Although my mother supported the church merger, most of my extended family did not. Many members could not separate the old building from their experiences of church— sorrow and joy, tears of repentance and grace, christenings, funerals, and weddings of family members and church family.

St. John's was a neighborhood church, and my Dad, in moods of reminisces, often said, "I don't know what we would have done without that little church." He was speaking of his brothers and sisters, his mother who was converted at age 38, and his father who became a member, settled down, and reared their family of seven in the church, which happened to be next door. My mother sustained her stance for the absorption of little St. John's into a larger and stronger witness by remembering what my father always said, "Someday the church will have to relocate in order to grow. Without a vision, the people will perish." My Dad never quoted any other Bible verse in my memory, but he spoke of "vision" when he discussed church and life through the years. He died in 1978, and the merger and its struggles came seven years later.

Members who couldn't stand the change joined other denominations or a small Methodist church north of Van Buren or one across the river in Fort Smith, or they stopped attending. My mother was hurt by their hurt and by the criticism she received for supporting this merger she held up to be "for the sake of those who come after me." She lived long enough to see a few of the old members eventually return, and long enough to sacrifice a lot of comforts to pay her extra pledges for the building fund. Only through the windows of memory, which scan the long benches on each side of the sanctuary, am I able to see the faces of the saints of St. John's, and I gain strength from these memories.

My strength now is quite different now compared to how I experienced it almost fifty years ago when I and fellow student council friends filled eight of the auditorium seats on the night of September 9, 1958. White Citizens Council (WCC) members were seated around us, as were other citizens, and, as I realized later, several reporters. On the stage the school superintendent and the school board members appeared, as demanded by the WCC. The exchanges of the factions have receded into the windowless vault of my memory, but I do remember raising my hand to ask permission to state results from our student poll. I remember the enthusiasm of the WCC and how it quickly turned into angry insults when they heard most students preferred integration to school closure.

I walked home that night with my closest cousin, Kay, a year ahead of me in school and the editor of the yearbook. I don't remember if either of us had asked for specific permission to attend the meeting. In general, I was allowed to attend school functions if they were within walking distance of my home. Out-of-town ball games were too much worry for my Dad who feared accidents and illness, fires and flash floods. I know some of the student council members got in BIG trouble with their parents for attending the meeting that night. The morning newspaper carried pictures of us with the story of our stand for integration. My husband, (then someone I barely knew, the boy in the striped shirt with a hand placed anxiously near his mouth in the September 22, 1958, issue of *Life* magazine) tells me he told his parents his intentions before the meeting. His Dad said, "O.K., this is your decision, but there's going to be trouble."

An avalanche of telegrams, mail, and repercussions of many sorts began the next day. The mail continued for more than a year, the repercussions longer. My parents' response to my stand for integration consisted of "you have a lot of mail again today" (my mother), and my Dad's two or three statements when referring to post cards from Las Vegas. These cards arrived at intervals, months apart but with the same handwriting, and they increasingly insisted I reverse my stand. "Those are death threats," he said. I didn't believe my Dad's interpretation of the postcards, but neither did I express my doubts, questions or feelings of any sort. Assassinations of white people who stood for integration did not occur, as far as I knew. Later, I learned differently.

Meanwhile, I felt little fear but a whole lot of loneliness. My loneliness came more from my parents' silence than from loss of friends or privileges. *Not* talking about family pain was a common characteristic of families in the 1950s, I think. Certainly, the '50s in Van Buren predated school counselors assigned to help students deal with feelings more painful than those related to college choices or interim coursework. Looking back, I think teachers and pupils, school officials and community persons may have offered me support and the opportunity to talk, but I was too uncomfortable with *any* mention of the topic of "my stand." I knew, although very quietly stated, if stated at all, that my parents did not want me in the spotlight, in plain sight for some stranger's agenda, good or bad. Personally, I deeply felt it would be wrong to receive benefit for doing something I knew the Holy Spirit's infusion had guided. I was to experience similar guidance at other times in my life, but the day and night of September 9, 1958 contained such a nearness of the Spirit that my actions unfolded as though they had been practiced for a lifetime, yet were completely new.

Preparation for the stand began the year before; this I realized almost immediately the day after my stand. I could trace this clear line of the Spirit's work. Early on, I was also aware of the influence of two pastors. One preached the first sermon I heard regarding the Christian response to integration soon after the Supreme Court's *Brown v. Board of Education* decision in 1954. The other pastor, Reverend William Wilder, was at St. John's when my stand occurred. Rev. Wilder took the full brunt of the repercussions. Now I am able to see thousands of impressions which propelled the direction of my stand. Then and now, I believe the idea of *how to take action* sprang from the Spirit's synthesis of my little bit of knowledge and deep conviction. A practical technique (the poll learned in a Student Council workshop at school the previous summer) and an inchoate desire to alleviate the crisis became a new creation. Although my sense of crisis had dead-locked my search for solutions, the Holy Spirit created order. Out of my desire and a small amount of knowledge He infused me with the inspiration for a plan of action.

I never doubted my action was right, a proper response to seeing people being mistreated. And I continued to believe the idea of *how* to take right action was mine alone, except for the help of the Holy Spirit. I reasoned that since the idea was mine alone, then no one but me should be hurt by it; and I didn't expect to be hurt much, if at all. By age fifteen, I had absorbed my parents' message that "if you try to do the right thing and do the best you can, things will work out just fine."

"Just fine" to me at the age of fifteen meant whatever outcome I might prefer. Now I know a deeper meaning, but then I was overwhelmed by the accumulation of mail and the accrual of other fall-out. In addition to reading the verbal insults in some of the letters that were addressed jointly to my parents and me, I was also seeing my parents' expressions when they answered the telephone. It helped me to receive affirmation for my stand from my sister and her husband in Connecticut, and it was good to know church members up there supported what my friends and I had done.

Foremost among the events for which I had no comfort was the news that my brother had been blacklisted from an organization he enjoyed very much. Then I learned my aunts were receiving hateful comments at meetings they attended, and even church members and life-long friends were making critical remarks to my parents. They didn't tell me any of this at the time. I overheard their low murmuring voices late at night. Guilt for their worry and the hurt of other family members weighed me down. Years later I realized they had to worry about our livelihood as well as about me and the rest of the family. The timing of the incident was terrible as far as their financial well-being was concerned.

My Dad had just left his full-time job, without any retirement. He was a little over fifty years of age. Since the age of sixteen, he had worked in a factory six days a week. When a financial need pressed too hard, he added "projects"—a saw mill or floor sweep production, a house construction, or the restart of a neighborhood grocery in the little building between our house and St. John's.

Tired a lot, he didn't speak with much animation unless with his siblings at family get-togethers or when at home discussing his favorite topics—the marvels of electricity, Horatio Alger-type stories, and the magnificence of the Constitution of the United States. "Everybody, no matter who they are, where they came from, or what color they might be, has the right to life, liberty and the pursuit of happiness," he would say with pride and happiness in his voice.

The house he and my mom worked on at night finally reached move-in condition when I was in the eighth grade. We were then three blocks from St. John's. By the time I entered the tenth grade, my Dad was finishing up correspondence school for television and radio repair. My Mom and I took turns running the little grocery store next to St. John's. When some customers became aware of "what the Evanses' daughter did," they stopped coming in. I worried someone would throw rocks through the plate glass window, but as far as I know that never happened. I learned later that some people deliberately became customers of the store as a way to offer support to my family.

Later, while reading books during my college years, I heard God called the "Numinous Other" in an author's attempt to describe His holiness and separateness from humankind; but as early as age three or four, I felt Him to be wholly with us. His presence completely filled the small sanctuary made golden by light from windows that were embedded with tiny lines which prevented outdoor views. Much of my awareness of Him came from my mother's shift to a different way of being when we began to climb the twenty concrete steps to the front doors of the church. By the top step, three times higher than me, she was in worship that didn't cease until we left the sanctuary and passed the swinging doors to the foyer.

I had been confirmed in the faith at age nine when I experienced repentance. Disconfirmation of my faith occurred off and on into early adulthood, not only because of the normal doubting that occurs in adolescence, but also through listening to pastors who preached what manuscripts "suggested" rather than what the Good News of the Gospel promised, or what Jesus' presence in their lives meant. My early foundation was strong. Between seven and fourteen, the preaching of Reverend Robert Paul Sessions challenged and deepened my Christian experience and that of many of us. It was not just Brother Bob's pulpit presence, but the quality of his caring which made real the claims of Christ. Brother Bob allowed teenagers, as well as adults, to express thoughts and concerns. Doubts could be described and explored. He told us about some of his experiences with Jesus, and he told us about things that were to come into our lives. Integration was one of these.

The experience of Brother Bob's caring, more than his impelling, added to my own capacity to care. The direction of my stand for integration had a foundation in his ministry, as well as my mother's saying, "Oh, I wonder how (someone) must be feeling." "Don't you know he/she must be (hurt, or sad, or upset) by this (some hardship)?" *How someone feels* became part my awareness and concern.

Reverend William Wilder came to St. John's in 1956 after Brother Bob moved. My pastor during my stand for integration, Rev Wilder made a significant impression on my life. One of his sermons contained the concept of "magnanimity." Rev. Wilder helped me understand that "unselfish" means more than passive sharing; it means active giving— the seeking out of those stranded in the byways and elevating them to the first place at the table. The meaning of this word and his life continue to call me. Not until the 1990s, when I listened to a man tell of the death of his wife from cancer, did the word achieve full vividness. Rev. Wilder told us magnanimity was open-handedness in giving and forgiving. The young widower described his wife as a young woman who ran toward life "with her hands held wide open." I saw more clearly that open-handedness allows us to fully receive and to enjoy, as well as freely give. During my own adult experiences of loss or discouragement or doubt, I am comforted by the memory of Rev. Wilder's faith, especially the grounding which anchors me when I remember the hymn he chose in the hardest of times: "The church's one foundation is Jesus Christ, her Lord." Each time I sing it, I more deeply realize He is truly the "author and finisher of our faith."

Some of St. John's members vocally opposed Rev. Wilder's defense of integration, harassing his family and him for their beliefs. Some church members sent food to the white boys as they picketed against integration at the school. I knew most of the boys on strike and some of their supporters. I knew the boys who attended my grade school had never liked school. I never perceived them to be particularly mean or hate-filled. In my view, these boys had hearts filled with the hope of "getting our school closed" because people had succeeded in closing the doors of Little Rock's Central High School rather than integrating. The boys perceived an advantage for themselves in our crisis, and advantage for themselves outran their concern for others.

At age fifteen, I was poorly equipped to handle the mail and phone calls which either requested me to say more for integration, or recant my stand. I deeply disliked the mail which contained charges that Communists controlled white liberals and people like me who were contributing to the weakening and death of our country. I did like the *New York Herald Tribune*'s September 13, 1958, front page story, "Segregation is not Christian." This and other publications posed my question of "How do you think it makes them feel" to the White Citizens' Council members who wanted the thirteen black children to leave our school. Now as an adult, I more clearly see that whipping up fears and pointing to conspiracies and plots often mask the fight for self-advantage.

Although comfort came from the compliments of people at school and church and via mail (which included letters from foreign missionaries saying my stand helped them convince people in their parts of the world that the Christian God loves everyone and is *for* them, not just for Americans or white people), I increasingly felt upset and confused, as well as guilty and alone. I was relieved we were experiencing a normal school year with its ball games and fun, but I was not having much fun.

Although my mother frequently said she was proud of all three of her kids, she rarely told us so individually. Not until 1984 when her broken hip forced a hospitalization, did I really know my mother was proud of me, specifically for my integration stand. Her hospital roommate happened to be a lady who introduced herself and then apologized for calling me names after my stand for integration. For months, the lady had come out of her house to call me names when she saw me walking by. To my mother she explained, "Back then I had hate in my heart, but now I'm a Christian. I'm different now, and I love everyone no matter their color, and I'm sorry for the way I used to be—and what I did."

My mother's reverence for God and concern for others contributed to my stand. My Dad's joy in the Constitution and belief in the rights and bright prospects for every individual convinced me that each of us, all of us, could progress. The preaching of gifted and caring pastors strengthened and guided my convictions. The nurture of the saints cultivated a desire for good for everyone. Little fragments of conversations, glances, and expectations helped equipped me. I believed I was valuable. I felt I had the right to privilege, even the privilege of making a difference.

As early as age six, I noticed the "separate but equal" elementary school designated for African Americans in Van Buren was separate but far from equal. Their building was ugly and had outdoor toilets, conditions the other two white elementary schools in town had overcome. In Van Buren, African American children rode a bus to attend junior high and high school in Fort Smith, thirty-five miles away. Some black families moved away in order to further their children's education, and some sent their children to live in a town with a high school. Some children ceased attending school altogether.

When I had occasion to ride the city bus to Fort Smith for violin lessons or to visit larger stores, I saw tired, silent people. Men, white and black, carried dome-shaped lunch boxes and wore overalls or khakis dirty from a day's work, but the men in the back of the bus laughed with each other. Lines of fatigue left their faces. As I grew older and learned more in school, I began to wonder if people who had survived slavery naturally possessed genes that endowed vitality to their descendants. While working with my husband as a missionary on an Indian reservation and other places where ethnics congregate without observation from members of a majority, I observed a talent for laughing, for enjoying the small events of living, and I've come to a conclusion: Ethnic people, because of marginalization or oppression, have learned "to hurry up and enjoy *now*" because tomorrow things may get worse.

Years later while living in Atlanta and completing my doctorate at Georgia Institute of Technology, I saw thousands of middle class homes whose owners and residents were African Americans. These neighborhoods were no different than those of middle-class whites. Some of the largest, most luxurious homes in Atlanta were owned by the few African Americans who had become wealthy. In Van Buren, I had seen African Americans living only on Pickett Hill or in a minor holler near 14th Street, and they appeared poorer than most of the white people, even though there were a lot of very poor white people. My children, who grew up in Atlanta, barely believed stories of separate water fountains for "whites" and "colored." They saw no reason for people to be separated into groups of white or black.

Today, people who have moved to the Van Buren area due to Hurricanes Katrina and Rita after never having lived outside the "projects" in Louisiana, have made it clear to my children, now in their 30s, that "class" (controlled by poverty, ignorance, oppression, and sin) creates great deficits in people, black and white. If poverty is a result of that oppression, the deficits ooze from great wounds. Oppression most surely devastates if parents have been brutalized and in turn brutalize their children. Cesspools of every kind of degradation describe some of the human habitations—not worthy to be called homes—that existed in the New Orleans projects before the hurricanes. Schools could not or did not make up the difference.

In late August 2006, I read a newspaper report that children in northern Louisiana had been segregated on the bus, with the African American children behind the white children. Such treatment stamps in the thoughts that "you're last," "you're behind all relevant others." I do not want to believe the intent was oppression, but whatever the intent, I know that slights smaller than this do not create a sense of ability and access. I don't believe Christians want to create second class citizens. All of us, oppressed and oppressors and silent observers who let it happen, will be hurt. While some of us find aggrandizement of self by having others "below us," this kind of pride is preyed upon by the powerful who are self-seeking. Economic exploitation of any group eventually costs everyone too much, I believe.

A current colleague in Fort Smith, where I work with people who are seriously and chronically mentally ill, including evacuees from the hurricanes, tells me certain towns in Arkansas are known to restrict the influx of African Americans. This colleague also sharply rebuked me for quoting verbatim my Auntie, born in 1899, who spoke of "Negroes." In the 1950s, such was the polite word, but I was horrified to realize that I had hurt him by even saying the word "Negro." I apologized and meant it. I more deeply realize labels associated with race, gender, sexual orientation, and national origin perpetuate lack of equality. Each of us desires to be known by name rather than by category.

I recognize that I am much more afraid of taking a stand now than when I was fifteen, and maturity has given me much more admiration and respect for those who preached justice when they knew it would bring certain trouble. I am grateful for all those who upheld love's injunctions even when the peace became disturbed and broken for the sake of making the circle larger. I also now recognize the tremendous power of caring and uncaring acts. Small acts of kindness, or disregard, appear impotent when I'm tired, but I am strengthened by the Scripture's injunction to nevertheless "cast our bread on the water." The return on these investments, like faith, is often unseen. Self-discipline and holy effort require more strength than I feel, frequently. I admire people who live out their faith with holy effort and self-discipline, never once receiving honor from the world's press or their church.

I know my stand required less of me than my sister's years of service to the world as a public school teacher. I know that life doesn't turn out "just fine" for many people who try very hard to do the right thing. I have learned that dark nights of the soul serve their purpose. I have learned that apology and remediation come years after only a moment of rejection and hate. Love given correctly never requires apology, and rejection and hate can be overcome. I know now that acts of courage, large or small, bring consequences as well as blessings; but, I increasingly recognize that the gifts of others, courageous or mundane, have blessed me beyond the givers' awareness or my thanks.

Today, surrounding the school auditorium, now empty of the seats where I and student council members stood up for integration, new buildings offer air conditioning and other modern conveniences. But years ago, before St. John's Church had a building in which to worship, trees provided shade for Sunday school classes begun as outreach to the Long Bell Community in Van Buren. Men, after full days of work, dug and walled a basement while women kept food supplied to them during these volunteer efforts after dark. Two more years of brick-laying and framing by church members built the sanctuary of Long Bell Methodist

Church/East Van Buren Methodist/St. John's Methodist Church, the neighborhood church which so blessed Mr. and Mrs. Jess N. Evans, Sr., and their children and grandchildren. Now, the merged successor, Heritage United Methodist Church, ministers to and through the grandchildren and even the great-great grandchildren of the first Evans to become part of the circle of fellowship in the Methodist Church in Van Buren, Arkansas.

Many commitments I need to keep are for the sake of those I will never know and the children who will come after me. These commitments at times seem to be of little importance and as inconvenient as holding Sunday school with only shade of a tree for air conditioning, but I continue to learn that the abundant life is in "seeing with eyes to see and ears to hear" the Spirit's prompts. I am convinced small acts of regard for others, like the loaves of bread, can be increased by God's grace, and I know love's injunctions continue to call me to action. Thanks be to God.

Hard Lessons Learned
William P. Boyer

It would be easy for me to write about the Civil Rights crisis in Arkansas Methodism with a tone of bitterness. Bitterness because of the way church leaders reacted to and criticized Wesley Foundation students and because of the time it took before there was any semblance of racial justice in The Methodist Church in Arkansas. It would also be easy for me to write with a tone of triumph. Triumph because of the bold stand the students of the Wesley Foundations across the state took at this critical juncture in history.

During the 1950s and 1960s, the hottest issue in Arkansas revolved around school integration. The issue was whether or not the state would continue its historic tradition of providing "separate but equal" public education for its African American population. Looking back now, the Eisenhower federalization of the Arkansas National Guard and the desegregation of Little Rock Central High School were painfully fresh on everyone's mind. Politicians, public and private school administrators, and religious leaders were being very careful of where they trod.

By about 1960, few Arkansas public schools were racially integrated. However, due to the federal courts, every state-supported institution of higher learning had at least made a token effort at racial integration on their campuses. Not so, however, for Methodist-supported Hendrix College in Conway. Its board of directors steadfastly dug in their heels and insisted that Hendrix maintain its tradition of whites only. Whenever this issue was raised, the two conferences in the Arkansas Methodist Church and the Hendrix board of directors would claim no racial prejudice by quickly pointing with pride to Philander Smith College in Little Rock. At that time, Philander Smith was admitting white students, but for all intents and purposes it was a "colored only" institution.

During this time, Dr. Albert Martin, Sr., was director of the Wesley Foundation at the University of Arkansas in Fayetteville and a board member at Hendrix College. He had made several attempts to persuade his fellow board members to admit colored students. His efforts, though, fell on deaf ears. The Hendrix board members also turned down a formal offer that would provide a full scholarship to the first African American student admitted to the college.

At that time, as in the present, most college campuses had an organization for Methodist students called Wesley Foundation or the Student Christian Association. Representatives from each Wesley Foundation throughout Arkansas would gather annually for the Foundation's state meeting. Each year the meeting was held on a different campus, with that campus having been selected by a vote of the students two years prior.

I was a student delegate to the state meeting the year it was held at Arkansas Polytechnic College in Russellville. I believe it was 1961. During that year's meeting, the issue concerning the Hendrix admission policy was the topic of discussion among the University of Arkansas's delegates, as it had been many times back on campus. We decided to present a resolution in a plenary session requesting that the Hendrix board of directors change the college's admission policy to include students of all races. I volunteered to draft the resolution and introduce it at the plenary session. We informed the president of the annual meeting of our intentions, and he offered suggestions on how the resolution should be phrased.

The time for the plenary session to begin finally arrived. I presented the resolution and moved for its acceptance. Gasps from several Wesley Foundation directors were heard throughout the room, but the student delegates raised little discussion or questions. The president called for a vote of the resolution. It passed with almost no opposition! As you probably can guess, opposition was raised by the delegates representing Hendrix College, but in the end, their arguments were thrown out.

Upon return to Fayetteville, I mailed copies of the resolution to the president of Hendrix College, the chairman of the board of trustees, and several of the state's larger newspapers. The *Arkansas Gazette* and the *Arkansas Democrat* ran front page articles about the resolution. The articles caused quite a stir. Reports have it that several parents of Hendrix students drove there with the intention of taking their children out of the college if it was going to integrate, though I don't believe any students actually left the college. Not long after that, those of us who had worked on the resolution received letters from a prominent Arkansas business man and a member of a Methodist Church. The letter's tone and content were not complimentary. We were called communists and nigger lovers and told that if we did not like the admission policy at Hendrix we should transfer to Philander Smith College.

As mentioned earlier, the location for the state meeting was selected two years in advance. The year after the state meeting in Russellville, the meeting was to be held at Philander Smith College. It would be that campus's first time to host the state meeting. Sometime after the state meeting concluded in Russellville, Wesley Foundation directors who attended the state meeting, fearing further complaints, voted to move the next year's meeting from Philander Smith to Henderson State Teachers College. Wesley Foundation student members took this as a slap in the face by Wesley Foundation directors and the church's leadership and a definite step backward in race relations.

Most of us involved with writing the resolution had graduated by the next year, so we did not attend the state meeting. I moved to Oregon to attend graduate school and did not regularly follow the events taking place in Arkansas. But all of us do remember the disappointment and the feelings of resentment toward the Wesley Foundation directors across Arkansas.

Charleston Makes History
Dale Bumpers

On May 4, 1954, the U.S. Supreme Court handed down a decision in the case of *Brown v. Board of Education* reversing the old *Plessy v. Ferguson* decision of 1896, which declared that "separate but equal" facilities for blacks was constitutional. At first, southerners only complained about it, not fully comprehending the magnitude of the decision. Even though the *Brown* decision stipulated that the change was to be carried out "with all deliberate speed," the mandate didn't seem to carry much urgency as far as southerners were concerned. There was a seeming sub rosa feeling that the court wasn't really serious and that somehow the whole thing could be finessed and given a little time. The nation was quiescent, and the South was routinely ignoring the decision.

Shortly after the *Brown* decision, Charleston school board members sought my advice on what course of action or inaction they should pursue. This was heavy stuff for the only lawyer in a one-horse town, three years out of law school and operating out of a cubicle in the back of the bank. I hadn't even read the *Brown* decision. My advice was made easy by the fact that both the board and the school superintendent were inclined to comply with the decision immediately. It was also made easy by the fact that I knew the decision had to be honored sooner or later, and I knew sooner would be easier. Obviously, the decision for Charleston could be delayed, "but the day of reckoning would come." Better to do it voluntarily than under a court order. When the Charleston newspaper got wind of the school board's decision to integrate, a small undercurrent of resistance emerged, but for the most part the reaction was amazingly tepid.

Charleston had about forty blacks, of whom twenty were children. Most of a once larger population had long since departed for Kansas City, Detroit, or Chicago. They had always lived two miles east of town in the "settlement" in shotgun hovels, trying to scratch out an existence on poor land. A few worked at the Acme Brick Plant in Fort Smith, hauling bricks in wheelbarrows to and from the kilns. They were the lucky ones.

The settlement consisted of a small African Methodist Episcopal church, sponsored by the Charleston Methodist Church in town, and a one-room schoolhouse where one teacher, paid by the Charleston School District, taught eight grades. The students in grades nine through twelve were bused to the all-black Lincoln High School in Fort Smith, twenty-four miles away.

When school opened that fall, thirteen black students got off school bus number two and walked unmolested, and virtually unnoticed, into the elementary and high schools. Charleston had become the only school in all of the eleven Confederate states to fully integrate its public schools in 1954. Two other schools in Arkansas had voted to integrate that fall, but the hostility of the people, once they found out about the votes, forced them to rescind the decisions.

Things were going smoothly. Initially, no black students tried out for basketball or football, but later, when they did, a number of schools refused to play Charleston. Two band contests in nearby communities also refused to allow Charleston's band to participate because of its black students. Instead of challenging the other schools, we made the black students stay home if the other schools objected. It took a lot of the luster off an otherwise compelling story of a courageous little community doing what was right. The second year, we stiffened our spines and insisted the black students participate in everything. The schools that had previously objected wilted.

In 1957, three years later, Little Rock's Central High School, the state's largest, began making elaborate preparations to accept nine carefully selected black students in the fall. Untold hours were spent attempting to assure a smooth opening day. The city was quiet, and there had been no organized opposition. Orval Faubus was in the first year of a second two-year term as Arkansas's governor. He had been a rather progressive governor and enjoyed a respectable approval rating. As the time neared for school to begin, a very few segregationists began to clamor for action to stop the "mongrelization" of the races. Their voices were loud but largely ineffective, though one person was watching and listening intently—Orval Faubus.

Faubus announced that the *Brown* decision was unlawful, and proceeded to call out the Arkansas National Guard to deny the nine black children admission to Central High. He, not the Supreme Court, would determine what constituted "equal protection" for black children in the future. On the morning of September 23, 1957, the nine black students marched up the beautiful curved steps of Central High School to its entrance where they were told by the National Guard commander that they would not be permitted to enter.

Well, the rest is history, and the only possible outcome ensued, but not until Faubus made a trip to confer with President Eisenhower. There was nothing to discuss, so Faubus returned home saying he had tried to resolve the matter. Eisenhower was slow to act and had to be convinced by his attorney general that he faced a constitutional crisis and had no choice. He was sworn to uphold the law, whether popular or not. Eisenhower sent home the National Guardsmen who were on duty at Central High School, and called in the Army's 101st Airborne Division from Fort Campbell, Kentucky. It is difficult, decades later, to understand that a major crisis was brewing and nobody could foresee a peaceful outcome. Until the 101st arrived, a mob that had been growing bigger and more unruly by the day was in control. People in Arkansas were frightened. Within three days of the 101st Airborne Division's arrival, the mob had totally disappeared.

At this time, Charleston Public Schools was entering its fourth year of peaceful desegregation. However, what had just happened at Central was spilling over into the town of Charleston. Some Charleston school board members were fanning the flames of resegregation. They had come up with a so-called plan that would meet any legal challenge and be without violence. The election to determine whether or not to resegregate was one of the most volatile and nasty elections in the school's history. After the votes were cast, Charleston Public Schools had kept its place in history as an integrated school.

Unfortunately, the hostility of the losing side in Charleston didn't end there. The night before school was to begin in 1958, the school superintendent and school janitor came to my home looking as if they had just seen the Holy Grail. They were pasty white with fear. The "diehards" had painted "nigger go home" in capital letters across the full width of the school, which faced the highway through town. We quickly recruited some help and scrubbed it off with turpentine and stiff-bristled brooms and hand brushes.

35

I went to the school the next morning and waited for who I thought were the perpetrators. Two of them drove by, and I have never seen faces more forlorn than theirs when they realized their handwork was gone. Only seven or eight people ever knew it had happened.

Editors' note:

The text above is an excerpt, used by permission, from former U. S. Senator Dale Bumpers' autobiography, The Best Lawyer in a One-Lawyer Town *(2004,University of Arkansas Press).*

A Minister's Daughter Remembers
Carol Beth Cade

The following is presented in honor of my parents, Reverend Charles David Cade and Hope Tabor Cade, in the Little Rock Conference of the Methodist Church in the 1930s and 1940s.

When I was a child of about three in Sparkman, Arkansas, around 1930, I was playing in the irises in our parsonage front yard when I saw two large feet near me just through the fence. As I looked up to see who it was, my eyes had to travel up and up to see the very tall, very black man standing there. I remember only that he asked me if my father was at home. When I was older, my mother told me that he was an African prince who had come to Sparkman to find descendants of his family who had been sold into slavery in the 1800s. He found them there. Members of the black community had sent him to see my parents. Mother invited him to eat supper with us the next night and also invited the presiding elder of our church.

In every charge my parents served, the black community knew it had a friend in them. Once when Dad was away and Mother was at home with their first child, she heard disturbing bird calls and knew it might be the Ku Klux Klan coming to punish my Dad. That had happened in our community, and members of the group knew where Dad stood on issues of race. Thankfully, the KKK did not arrive.

Later in Murfreesboro, Arkansas, when I was about seven, Mother worked together with two black school teachers there to plan a Vacation Church School in the black Methodist church. She drew in members of our white Methodist church to take part. At the end of the closing program, the children made a circle in the alter area to sing "The World Children for Jesus." The two-year-old daughter of one of the white women who had helped with the program, broke away from her mother, ran up and joined hands with the black children, a moving testimony to the rightness of the event.

In each church they served, Mother, through the Women's Society, planned a World Day of Prayer service in which both races took part. It was the young people, black or white, who seemed to value this most, singing together in the choir.

My parents were not activists in the sense of the later Civil Rights era. Dad simply preached that we could not be truly Christian unless we dealt with all men as our brothers. And he lived it. He was sometimes asked to take part in a funeral for a black community member alongside the black pastor, and sometimes drove members of the bereaved family to the church for the service. When mother had household help, she often worked alongside of that help and made lunch for them to eat together. Their congregations knew of this, and at least one prominent member of a congregation asked the bishop to move them, which the bishop did.

In Pine Bluff, in the late 1940s, my mother and the wife of the Episcopal minister were members of the Council of Church Women, which bought and renovated a small building. It replaced a ramshackle house on the edge of town that was a home for indigent and elderly black women. To add an interesting dimension to my mother's actions, it is relevant to note that her maternal and paternal grandparents had been slave holders in Georgia and Mississippi. She was eligible to join both the United Daughters of the Confederacy and the Daughters of the American Revolution, but joined neither, even though urged by an aunt to do so.

John Miles, a minister in the Little Rock conference, and Hendrix classmate of mine, followed my dad to three different charges, and knew what his ministry was like. At my dad's funeral, which I asked John to lead, John read a written request from my dad, who had planned his own service. It asked that nothing be added or taken away from his plans. John said, "I am sorry, Charlie, but I have something to add." He told it like it was. Charlie, he said, had served some of the most difficult churches in the conference, and he described some of the work that my father had done in them.

Dad was not an Arkansas native and was dubbed a Modernist by some of his peers. He saw his service as a commitment first to do the will of God as he saw it. He would not approve of my writing this, but I'm sorry Charlie, the world needs to know what you and your wife, Hope Tabor, accomplished in your very quiet way years before the Civil Rights movement.

Raising Up Leaders for the Kingdom:

Arkansas Methodist Involvement in the Struggle for Racial Integration of Van Buren High School*

Michael G. Cartwright

A rguably, nothing has had a more determinative effect on the shape of the mission of Methodism in American culture than racial segregation. From the days of when Richard Allen and company were pulled from their knees at Historic Old St. George's Methodist Episcopal Church in Philadelphia, to the evacuation of United Methodist churches in urban areas in the 1970s and 1980s, the history of segregated Methodism is a familiar, if sad, story. Within that larger story, the era of the Civil Rights struggle (1954-1965) stands out as one of the times when the Methodist Church in America faced new kinds of challenges to its segregationist practices, from within as well as outside the denomination. In retrospect, it also can be seen as an era in which the mission of the Methodist Church began to be reshaped in significant ways. Indeed, the decade of 1955-1965 was an extraordinary time not only for American culture but also for the Methodist Church.

Strangely enough, to date, the story of the involvement of Methodist church leaders in the Civil Rights Movement has not been told. While others have told the story of the struggle in individual congregations[1] during this era, and the efforts of particular (African American) Methodist leaders in the Civil Rights struggle[2] and more recently, the role of such groups as the National Council of Churches,[3] to date, no one to my knowledge has attempted to chart the involve-

---

*For several reasons, not the least of which is the unavailability of documents and oral history sources, this paper is limited to the role of "white Methodists" in the integration struggle. Although I strongly suspect that some African American Methodists in north Arkansas may have been involved, directly and indirectly, in the events narrated in this paper, I have been unable to ascertain anything about the role played by African American Methodists who at that time would have been part of the Southwest Conference of the Central Jurisdiction. The fact that the color line continues to shape reporting of these events is one of the more poignant reminders of the unresolved legacy of racism in the United States of America, The United Methodist Church in general, the state of Arkansas, and the North Arkansas Conference in particular.

39

ments of Methodist church leaders in the Civil Rights Movement at what might be called the intermediate level; namely, what were the predominantly Euro-American Methodist conferences in the South doing individually and corporately as Methodists during the integration struggle? What follows provides a modest beginning of that effort by recounting how north Arkansas Methodist clergy and laity *did and did not* offer leadership in the integration struggle between 1955 and 1965.

This episode reflects the corporate struggle of the North Arkansas Conference to face the challenge posed, for Methodist congregations and institutions, as well as the wider set of communities within which Methodist leaders also participated, by the court-ordered integration of public schools beginning with the May 1954 Supreme Court ruling on *Brown v. Board of Education of Topeka.*

To attempt to narrate the history of north Arkansas Methodist involvement in the integration struggle is to confront the manifold ways in which these events intersect with other narratives—the story of state (Arkansas) and regional (southern) identity, the story of "Southern Methodism" in relation to the wider connection of the Methodist Church, the story of the Central Jurisdiction, the story of an evolving church-college relationship, and arguably the story of the eclipse of "connectionalism" in the Methodist Church, the story of the beginnings of the process of membership loss and the narrative about denominational decline. Obviously, it is not possible to narrate all of these strands, but they should at least be noted at the outset, for in various ways they contribute to the story of why north Arkansas Methodists not only struggled with integration, but also struggled *with one another* in facing the challenge that integration of schools and colleges posed for their congregations and conference.

I. North Arkansas Methodist Conference Actions: 1952-1958

On paper, as the decade of the 1950s commenced, the Methodist Church was on record as clearly standing *against* racial discrimination. For example, the 1948 *Book of Discipline* contained an important resolution on "The Christian Church and Race," which forthrightly stated:

> The principle of racial discrimination is a clear violation of the Christian belief in the fatherhood of God, the brotherhood of man,

and the Kingdom of God, the proclamation of which in word and life is our gospel. We therefore have no choice but to denote it as unChristian and to renounce it as evil. *This we do without equivocation.*[4]

In practice, however, racial discrimination suffused the very structure of the Methodist Church in general and Arkansas Methodists in particular. Within the larger connection the Central Jurisdiction ensured that there was limited contact between African American and Euro-American Methodists, and within the state of Arkansas, the segregation of the churches in the Southwest Conference from the North Arkansas and Little Rock Conferences served to ensure the pursuit of separate missions in Arkansas Methodism. Yet, the North Arkansas Conference, which was located in the "northern" section of one of the southern states known for being "moderate," was notably "moderate" in its dealings with race relations in the late 1940s and early 1950s. Little Rock, a city known for its "relatively progressive attitude toward race relations,"[5] was located just south of the boundary of the conference.

It would appear that *Brown v. Board of Education* was the event that prompted North Arkansas Methodists to become involved in the corporate sense of engaging the struggle for integration. As the Reverend William M. Wilder recalls: "we were not very aware of the problems concerning race relations."[6] Conference records from 1948 to 1954 suggest that very little in the way of official action took place within the North Arkansas Annual Conference of the Methodist Church.[7] A report in the 1952 Conference Journal noted that "C. C. Neale of the Colored Methodist Episcopal Church was introduced to the Conference and it was announced by the Bishop that Brother Neale will be in the vestibule following the session for the purpose of receiving an offering for his summer program for colored pastors."[8] The image of a C. M. E. minister standing hat-in-hand outside the conference precincts stands as a poignant reminder not only of segregated Methodism, but also of the lack of concern for race relations. At that time, "Race Relations Sunday" (celebrated annually on the Second Sunday of February) was celebrated by some Methodist pastors and congregations and ignored by others.

However, this should not be taken to mean that there were no initiatives within the conference. Here and there tentative contacts were made between ministers across racial lines. Some of the ministers involved in these early cross-racial contacts had been trained at Perkins School of Theology, at Southern Methodist University in the late 1940s and early 1950s, at a time when the administration of the seminary came under fire from students and others for its segregationist policies. African Americans were allowed to audit some courses, but they were not allowed to enroll in the seminary. In 1948 and 1949, student protests occurred at Perkins. Discussions with students and faculty at this seminary, led to the decision by the Board of Trustees of Perkins School of Theology in 1950 to integrate the seminary. Perkins would be the first Methodist-related seminary in the southern United States to admit African Americans.[9] Charles McDonald, a ministerial student from the North Arkansas Conference, was a student at Perkins the year the decision was made to integrate the seminary. By the time Jim Beal, another ministerial student from the North Arkansas Conference, enrolled at Perkins in the fall of 1952, the seminary had been integrated. Beal's class included Cecil Williams, Negail Riley and several other African American Methodists who would become prominent leaders in the United Methodist Church.

An examination of North Arkansas Conference records suggests that there was a discernible increase in the attention being given to race relations in general, and to integration in particular, beginning with the 1954 Conference year. The 1954 *Journal of the North Arkansas Conference* reported that special offerings had increased in all but three areas; one of those three areas was "Race Relations" and another was "World-Wide Communion." If this decline is one indicator that grassroots support for race relations was tepid at best, there were also a few modest examples of interracial cooperation. For example, early in 1954, Charles McDonald, pastor of First Methodist Church in Ozark, invited African American Christians from area churches to a joint worship service at the Ozark church, an event which was well-received by all those involved. While this may not have been the first integrated worship experience in the North Arkansas conference, it is an example of the limited exploratory ventures that were being explored at that time by Methodist pastors sympathetic to integration.[10]

The 1954 *Journal* also notes that at the Annual Conference session held in Batesville, Charles McDonald read the report of a new "Social and Economic Relations" committee, and it was adopted by the conference as a whole by a standing vote, but for some reason it was not included in the reports of that *Journal*.[11] Although the journal listed the document as included, it was not. It is not immediately clear why this omission occurred, but there is some suspicion that the report may have been dropped by the leadership of the conference (at least some of whom were known to be against integration) in an attempt to squelch some of the more "radical" young ministers like Beal and McDonald.[12] Although no known copy of this report survives, Robert Paul Sessions would later report in a letter addressed to Dr. Marshall T. Steel, at that time President of Hendrix College, that "on June 19, 1954, the North Arkansas Annual Conference adopted a report (by a standing vote), by its Board of Social and Economic Relations welcoming the Supreme Court decision on integration as *"a reflection of the Christian ideal," and calling on our people to pray and work 'with varying timeliness' for the achievement of that ideal in all areas of life, including the institutions of the church.*"[13]

In retrospect, this action, taken less than five weeks after the landmark *Brown v. Board of Education of Topeka* decision of the U. S. Supreme Court, also marks the beginning of a new approach for the North Arkansas Conference to the traditional concern about "brotherhood" and "race relations." For the first time in the history of the annual conference, integration was identified as an "ideal" to be realized by North Arkansas Methodist church leaders in all institutions related to the church. While the resolution *did not specify* what "integration" would mean for the conference structure as a whole, or the districts, local churches and charges of which it was comprised, it was a suggestive if strategically qualified agenda for struggle. But as the strange "disappearance" of this document also suggests, North Arkansas Conference church leaders were not yet ready or willing to follow the implications of this resolution, nor were people in the churches of the conference ready to engage in the struggle at the local level.

II. The Struggle to Integrate Van Buren High School: September 1958

While delegates to the 1957 and 1958 sessions of the North Arkansas Conference may have had some inkling about what would transpire at nearby Central High School in Little Rock, Arkansas, in the coming months, they could hardly have foreseen that two north

Arkansas Methodist church leaders, a pastor and the president of the Methodist Youth Fellowship in a local church, would provide critical leadership in the integration struggle at Van Buren High School in the fall of 1958, and in so doing, "teach, preach, and practice Christian love and brotherhood."

In the wake of the 1954 landmark U. S. Supreme Court decision, *Brown v. Board of Education*, parents and guardians of Van Buren African American students had filed a suit in federal court in 1955 asking for desegregation of the high school. An agreement had been reached between parents and the school board and a nine-year integration plan, proposed by the school board, had been accepted. The first stage in the plan, integration of the Van Buren High School, was scheduled to go into effect in the fall of 1957. Prior to the start of integration, African American students had attended Lincoln Senior High School (a "Negro school") in Fort Smith, Arkansas. The lawsuit was subsequently dismissed by Federal District Judge John E. Miller, who cited the Van Buren school board's positive action toward integration (as demonstrated in the agreement reached with Negro parents) as a warrant for his ruling.

In light of subsequent events, it is somewhat amazing to realize that, unlike Central High School in Little Rock, Van Buren High School had been integrated *without significant incident* in the fall of 1957. Twenty-four African American students had enrolled in September 1957. One African American student was graduated from Van Buren High School in the spring of 1958. Several other high schools (Fayetteville, Bentonville, Charleston) in northwest Arkansas and Hoxie in northeastern section of the state (the sections of the state where the largest number of integrated schools emerged in 1957-58) also integrated without incident. Controversy in these Arkansas public schools would not emerge until the *second* year of integration, when it became clear what the Supreme Court's response to the Central High School appeal for delay of execution of the court's 1954 ruling would be.

When the Van Buren High School opened on Tuesday, September 2, 1958, thirteen African American boys and girls walked through the doors of the school, only to encounter the embodiment of the message that they were not welcome back from their summer vacation. In the words of *The New York Times*: "They marched past jeering white youths and derisive inscriptions painted on sidewalks and brick walls of buildings."[14] As the week wore on, opposition to integration mounted. Negro students were jeered as they arrived for classes on the second day of the school year. There were also reports of injuries, of an African American student and his grandmother, although these were never confirmed.

Early on Thursday, September 4, the white students gathered at a garage building on a corner across from the Van Buren senior high school. A spokesperson for the group announced that forty-one boys had organized a strike to resist integration, and indicated that their group would not return to class until Negroes were permanently removed. According to some reports, some of the strikers alluded to the possibility that they might use force "if necessary" to return the school to an all-white status.[15] One of the student strikers was quoted as telling a reporter: "Our parents approve of what we are doing…" During the day, cars were parked across the street from the school with signs that read "niggers go home, whites will come back" and "chicken whites go to school with jigs."[16] Ten people who were not students joined the student strikers during the morning hours. Only two Negro students, both girls, were reported to have attended classes on Thursday.

One of the first acts taken by the group of student strikers was to attempt to contact Gov. Orval E. Faubus seeking support for their strike. When they were unable to contact the governor by telephone, they elected to send a telegram. The telegram read: "In behalf of Van Buren High School we are on strike here. In order to stay integration we need your help." The message was signed "Roger Williams," a name which later reports would indicate did not appear on the list of enrolled students at Van Buren High School.[17] The governor's public response to the telegram was noncommittal. Local school officials also did not offer any comment about the student strike.

Later on Thursday evening, a group of white students gathered around the flagpole at the high school where they burned a Negro in effigy. According to the Associated Press report:

> Tonight a group of students burned a Negro in effigy on the flag pole of the high school… The students took a dummy from the trunk of an automobile and set it afire despite the yells of a guard atop the school building. The guard threatened to shoot. The dummy flared for a few minutes. It set afire the grass at the base of the flag pole and the demonstrators stamped out the flames on the ground but let the effigy burn to charred rags.[18]

The AP wire service report assessed the event this way: "The students seemed more bent on having a lark than creating a serious integration problem in burning the effigy."[19] Significantly, this event was not reported in the local press.

At about the same time, a group of forty-five adults, most of whom were parents of the student strikers, met at a downtown restaurant to discuss their sons' strike against integration. One woman, who opened the meeting, was quoted as saying, "The kids took the first step today, now it is up to us."[20] Numerous participants expressed their frustration about the roles played by the high school principal, Calvin Patterson, the school board and school superintendent Everett Kelley. Some persons voiced the desire to "close the school" apparently with the intention of starting a private school, but this proposition was dropped after another participant pointed out that the cost of operating a private school would be prohibitive. The meeting appeared to lack focus, according to newspaper reports. Some participants apparently quoted from the Christian Bible, claiming "these [Bible passages] show that the Supreme Court's law is wrong."[21]

Apparently some persons were present who attempted to moderate extremist views. One person in particular was identified in newspaper reports as being the "pastor of a Van Buren church" who called for "level-headedness on this problem" and disputed the way participants were interpreting the Bible in support of segregation. William M. Wilder, the pastor of St. John's Methodist Church in Van Buren, recalls attending that meeting, along with the Reverend Mr. Vernon Schmidt, pastor of the local Presbyterian Church. Wilder and Schmidt attended with the intention of trying to prevent those present from engaging in more militant action than they otherwise might attempt in the absence of members of the clergy. Apparently this strategy succeeded, at least in part, because not much action was taken at the meeting, and those persons who were initially elected to lead the group were "moderates," at least compared to some of the more mean-spirited white supremacists present at the gathering. Wilder would later recall: "I think it really bothered them when we showed up. I do not recall talking much, but I doubt if I kept my mouth shut! Probably Schmidt talked about being level-headed, although he wanted to keep quiet because he was a Yankee!"[22] Subsequently, it was reported in the local press that the group of parents/supporters had elected a board on Thursday evening. The Friday morning September 5th edition of the *Southwest American* newspaper reported: "there were no acts of violence or outward demonstrations on Thursday...."[23] It is not clear whether the newspaper ignored the effigy incident or simply did not know about it, but I have not been able to find any record of this event having been reported in the Van Buren/Fort Smith media.

None of the thirteen African American students enrolled at Van Buren high school attended classes on Friday, September 5, (the fourth day of school) and for a while it appeared that the student strikers were gaining support. According to one news report, "about a dozen girls joined the strikers Friday morning" but the Associated Press wire service reported that the total number of strikers was reduced from forty-eight to forty-four students. A second telegram was sent to Governor Orval Faubus requesting his assistance in the anti-integration effort.[24]

Also on Friday, a "committee of four local Negro leaders" met with the superintendent of schools, Everett Kelley. Afterward, the committee reported that Kelley "assured the committee that the school officials were doing all they could but that doesn't seem to be very much."[25]

At this point in the Van Buren integration struggle, it became known that student participants in the boycott who *returned* to classes would have to be accompanied by their parents, an announcement that parents of the student strikers regarded as contemptible, but which the superintendent of schools interpreted as standard policy. According to *The New York Times*, "Several adults, who identified themselves as parents of some of the striking students, brought refreshments to the group on the corner and encouraged them to continue their boycott."[26] At least one of the people who provided refreshments to the boycotters was a member of St. John's Methodist Church in Van Buren.

By Saturday, September 6, the African American leadership in Van Buren had been mobilized for action. The regional counsel of the National Association for the Advancement of Colored People (NAACP) conferred with Van Buren Negro leaders about possible court action to enforce integration at Van Buren high school. The NAACP field secretary for the five-state southwest region issued a statement at Van Buren on Saturday afternoon declaring that the school situation "must be placed at the doorsteps of Governor Orval

Faubus and his program of racial mischief and massive resistance to school integration."[27] As it happened, Governor Faubus also made his first public statement on Saturday afternoon, indicating that he did not plan to take any action in the matter of the student strike at Van Buren high school. Faubus commented: "The information that I get is that the situation gives every indication of quieting."

Over the weekend, rumors circulated throughout the community, on both sides of the color line. One local African American leader was quoted in the local press as having a "wait and see" attitude. Parents of the thirteen Negro children were advised by NAACP leadership to keep their children studying school texts so that when they were given the opportunity to attend class, they would not fall far behind. And members of the (all-white) school board maintained their silence about the controversy, a circumstance which appears to have been interpreted in widely different ways depending on one's own moral and political position on the issue of integration. Some persons suspected the board to be sympathetic to the student strikers, while some parents of the boycotting students believed that the board was "pro-integration."

Meanwhile, white pastors of Van Buren area churches were quoted as having commented on the integration struggle in their Sunday sermons: The Reverend William M. Wilder, pastor of St. John's Methodist Church in Van Buren, and president of the city's Ministerial Alliance addressed the issue in a sermon on "The Oneness of God."[28] In a Monday morning front page article entitled "Without Mentioning Integration, V. B. Ministers Counsel Flocks," the *Southwest American* newspaper quoted Wilder as proclaiming: "Democracy is a rule of the majority, but it is the function of the majority to protect the rights of the minority.... Moral problems are matters for the human conscience and not something to be decided by a poll of people."

Wilder's sermon drew a strong contrast between God's will and the demagogic manipulation of popular opinion.[29] In addition to what the newspapers reported, Wilder asked his congregation to consider the following (rhetorical) question(s): "Was Jefferson right when he stated that the principle of American democracy is that it must be a function of the majority to protect the rights of the minority—or shall [w]e go back to the godless rule of an Israel that was destroyed because 'every man did what was right in his own eyes'?" In effect, Wilder was calling upon his congregation to distinguish between that conception of majority rule which, supported white privilege, and implicitly white supremacist ideology, and a conception of democracy that was more radical precisely because it was directed by a conception of prophetic Christianity.

With the beginning of the second week of classes on Monday, September 8, it was still unclear what direction the student strike would take. This confusion is reflected in the contemporaneous press reports, some of which described the strike as spreading, others of which represented the boycott of classes as dwindling.30 That same day, the regional counsel for the NAACP filed a petition seeking a contempt citation against Van Buren senior high school officials. The attorney for the NAACP then went to Harrison, Arkansas, to ask for a temporary restraining order against the school board in Van Buren's integration controversy. This request was denied by Judge Miller, who also suggested that the NAACP attorney file a new lawsuit, the proper legal procedure in this case.

On Monday evening, the Van Buren Citizens Group that had organized itself on the previous Thursday, met again to decide how to proceed in presenting their grievances to the local school board (which was scheduled to meet the next evening). At this meeting, a new chairman was elected and a new board was established, as two of its officers had resigned in less than a week.

In another significant development, the Chief of Police issued a prepared statement to the press on Monday afternoon in which he made explicit his own support for the student strikers. The chief drew a parallel between striking Van Buren high school students and the participants in the Boston Tea Party of 1775, commenting that in both instances American people were fighting for what they thought was right. For this reason, the chief of police argued that the striking students should not have "to crawl back" to the school by making apologies for their behavior.

While the police chief claimed not to be condoning the student pickets, he added that students "were doing nothing illegal and were picketing in an orderly manner..." He added that anyone doing anything illegal would be thoroughly investigated and that anyone who engaged in destructive violence would be dealt with severely. At the same time, he observed that the total property damage from the previous week's disturbances probably would amount to "no more than $10," including the damaged caused by smearing paint on school buildings.

As of Monday evening, with the announcement of the chief of police's support, the student strike could still have succeeded, especially given the silence of the local school board about their intentions. With the apparent abdication of leadership of the school board and the police chief's support of Van Buren's version of the White Citizens Council, the integration struggle had made clear that there was also a leadership vacuum in the community of Van Buren. None of the civic leaders of the community was prepared to step forward to support integration. As elsewhere in Arkansas, the leadership of the city of Van Buren was anxiously awaiting what the U.S. Supreme Court would decide in the appeal of Central High School.

At this juncture two events occurred, independently of one another, which would significantly alter the outcome of the integration struggle at Van Buren High School. Interestingly enough, both of these actions directly involved Methodist church leaders from the (all Euro-American) St. John's Methodist Church. The leadership provided by Angie Evans, who at that time was the president of the youth group at St. John's church, and Bill Wilder, the pastor of the church, would turn out to make the difference in the Van Buren integration crisis.

First, on Tuesday, September 9, Reverend William M. Wilder responded to the chief of police's comments with a stinging rebuke. "Now I know—the police condone the actions of this unruly band of boys." Wilder also refuted the chief's comparison of the students' actions to the Boston Tea Party, saying, there was "no comparison." Wilder added, "The truth is that so far lawlessness and violence have won out in Van Buren with the acknowledged support of those pledged to keep the law." At the invitation of the local newspaper, the chief of police responded to Wilder's remarks by appearing to disregard them, only commenting that "everybody has a right to their opinion."[31]

In effect, Wilder's rebuttal had *neutralized* the chief's assertions in support of the student boycotters, by calling attention to the fact that his patriotic appeal to American saga of freedom from oppression was but a "cover story" for the police chief's failure to do his job to preserve order in the town. In a circumstance where the citizenry of Van Buren was already on edge, Wilder succeeded in putting the police chief on the defensive about how well he was doing his job.

On Tuesday evening, the Van Buren Citizens group brought its grievances to the regular monthly meeting of the Van Buren School Board, which took place in the auditorium of the Van Buren Senior High School. A spokesman for this group asked: "We know the Negro students don't have a decent school of their own, but can we get them back into Lincoln (Fort Smith Negro high school) and what are the chances of building a school here?" He also objected to the school policy of requiring returning student strikers to sign papers to get back into school. (Apparently, implicit in this action was the requirement that the students in question must "walk the straight and narrow" henceforth). Superintendent Kelley's response to this query was to remind the Citizens group that this was a standard procedure for students who had been absent from classes.

Also appearing before the school Board that evening was Jessie Angelina "Angie" Evans, a fifteen-year old junior, who had just begun serving as the president of the Van Buren Senior High School Student Council after the person elected to serve was disqualified. Throughout the previous week, Ms. Evans had quietly but purposefully rallied other student leaders in an attempt to maintain calm inside the 635-pupil school. Later officials of Van Buren High School would credit Angie and her group of student leaders with having done much to keep down the tension among white pupils inside the school who were trying to ignore jeering boycotters outside the windows of their classrooms. When it became clear that the Tuesday evening meeting would be the scene of a showdown between parents of the students boycotting classes and the school board, Angie Evans and her peers took quick and decisive action. Believing that "Negroes have a right to attend school just as much as anybody" and convinced that most of their peers would agree,[32] Angie and a small group of students took a poll of students at Van Buren High School in the three hours prior to the Tuesday night meeting.

When it was her turn to speak, Angie Evans made her surprise announcement: a poll had been taken in the school Tuesday afternoon. Of the 160 students who were polled, eighty-five thought it was only fair that the Negro students attend the school, thirty didn't care either way, and forty-five were opposed to integration. Angie concluded her report with a statement urging that integration proceed as planned. "We think it is only fair that the Negroes be permitted to attend this high school ... If we don't object why should anyone else? ... Have you thought what you make those Negro children feel like, running them out of school?"[33] Angie Evans went on to comment that the student strikers were disorderly, used abusive language and had painted and exhibited abusive posters. At this point, several irate parents of student strikers interrupted to charge that Evans and Kay Kincheloe (editor of the high school yearbook) had been "coached" (by school officials) on what to say at the school board meeting, a charge which both students denied emphatically. Ms. Evans' response at this point was simple but firm: "I just don't think segregation is a Christian thing."[34]

After hearing both sets of complaints, the school board went into executive session without taking any action at all, leaving approximately one hundred Van Buren residents in the auditorium discussing the integration controversy in separate groups. The school board had taken no action, but as subsequent events would make clear, acting independently, Angie Evans and Bill Wilder had managed to stem the tide of resistance to integration, and over the course of the next two weeks the tide would turn. In retrospect, the events of Tuesday, September 9, turn out to have been the decisive confrontations in the struggle to keep Van Buren High School integrated, although the NAACP and others would continue their legal efforts against the school board.[35] By Monday, September 22, the struggle had come to an end, just three weeks after it had begun. On that day, eight of the original thirteen African American students returned to classes at Van Buren High School.[36] The crisis was over.

III. Telling the Story After the Struggle Is Over: 1958-1959

For Angie Evans and Rev. Bill Wilder, however, the deluge had just begun. In the weeks to come both would receive an unusually large volume of mail, with the greater part of it going to Ms. Evans. Angie's simple but forthright response to the challenge of the Citizens Council on the occasion of the school board meeting appears to have prompted the outpouring of response that she received from across the world. Wilder received support and criticism not only for the support that he gave to

Angie Evans but also for his rebuke of Chief Russell's maladroit attempt to invoke the patriotic example of the Boston Tea Party in support of the student boycott of Van Buren High School. In due course, a five-hundred dollar grant from the Currier Foundation in New York would be awarded to Wilder (through the local church) in recognition of the leadership he gave in the Van Buren integration struggle.

A. Secular Media Portrayals: However, Angie Evans' role in the events of Tuesday, September 9, is what appeared to attract the interest of the national media. Angie Evans was the subject of several articles in nationally distributed magazines and newspapers over the course of the next few weeks. Associated Press wire service reports focusing on Angie Evans, including an Associated Press article, were printed in newspapers throughout the country on Thursday, September 11, and Friday, September 12. A related article appeared in the *New York Herald-Tribune* on Saturday, September 13, immediately beneath stories about the U.S. Supreme Court's decision that Central High School must integrate without further delay. This particular article appears to have struck a chord on a weekend when much of the nation was uncertain how Governor Orval Faubus would proceed in the face of the court order.

Such newspaper articles as these would subsequently provide the basis for articles in *Newsweek*, *Time*, *Life*, *Look*, *Jet* and other national-distributed magazines. Several of these articles, called attention to Angie and her family as "members of St. John's Methodist congregation" and noted that recent pastors[37] of that congregation were known to preach from the pulpit that "racial crises can best be solved by Christian principle."[38] Shortly after the publication of the articles in the *New York Herald-Tribune*, *Time*, and *Newsweek*, Ms. Angie Evans was overwhelmed by "an avalanche of congratulatory mail"[39] from all around the state as well as the throughout the U.S.A. and several foreign countries. At the end of the *Look* article she is portrayed as modest and wanting to "slip back into her former anonymity."

B. Church-Related Perspectives: Articles in the secular press were followed quickly by pieces in various Protestant denominational publications such as the Methodist Church's *Together*, a devotional resource for Methodist families published by the Methodist Publishing House in Nashville, Tennessee. For months thereafter, Ms. Evans would receive letters from Methodist Youth Fellowships as well as non-Methodist[40]

53

youth groups from around the country. During this same time period, Methodist officials in Arkansas demonstrated their support of Angie's actions in various ways. According to denominational newspapers, acting on behalf of Bishop Martin and the North Arkansas Conference district superintendents, the Reverend Ethan W. Dodgen presented Angie with a leather-bound edition of the Bible. The presentation read, in part, "To a girl of high courage and fine Christian convictions."[41]

Scores of pastors, Sunday school teachers, and conference officials from all over north Arkansas wrote letters of support to Angie Evans and Bill Wilder. Several writers imagined Angie Evans' actions in terms of Isaiah's prophecy of the Peaceable Kingdom, particularly the image of Isaiah 11:6: "...*and a little child shall lead them.*"[42] In retrospect, this comment seems rather extravagant, and may say more about the Methodist yearnings for moral heroes at the time than it did about Angie Evans. To be sure, some of the remarks about this particular text were marked by sentimentality, and more than a few assumed more intentionality on Evans' part than was the case. Nevertheless the very attempt to frame her actions in the context of biblical prophecy displayed the efforts of these Arkansas Methodists church leaders to see the significance of this young woman's actions in the context of the Kingdom of God. Not all of the letters from Methodists were supportive however. Some vigorously attacked Wilder and Evans for their "unChristian" support of integration, and more than a few expressed the hope that they would live to regret what they had done in the integration struggle. These responses make clear that the division between proponents of integration and advocates of segregation existed *within* the Methodist churches in north Arkansas, as well as within the state of Arkansas as a whole. For in fact, at the grassroots-level Methodist congregations in Arkansas were very much divided about integration, not only with respect to questions of public policy but also with respect to proposals for integration within the fellowship of the Methodist Church and its institutions of higher education.

As the subsequent effort by Arkansas Methodists to integrate Hendrix College would illustrate, however inspiring Isaiah's vision of the peaceable Kingdom of God might be for those church leaders who supported integration, practical questions of leadership in conference, collegiate and local church continued to vex north Arkansas

Methodists as they found themselves in conflict with one another. Nevertheless, in the midst of trying to discover ways forward, more than a few church leaders continued to keep the faith, trying to discern the Kingdom of God through the strife of the struggle. They found inspiration and courage in the fact that God had "raised up" leaders in their midst, clergymen like the Rev. William M. Wilder and laypeople like Ms. Angie Evans, who somehow found the courage to stand up for Christian principles in the context of the struggle to keep Van Buren High School integrated.

Conclusion

Earlier in this article, I gestured to the multiplicity of narratives that intersect in the midst of attempting to offer a chronicle of Methodist involvement in the Civil Rights movement. One of the narrative threads that would be well worth following would be how these displays of moral courage by clergy and laity fit into the Methodist tradition's practice of discerning God providential interventions in human history through the lives of ordinary people. Reflecting the biblical imagery of the Old and New Testaments, John Wesley and the early Methodists spoke with humility and awe about the capacity of God to "raise up children of Abraham" to serve God's kingdom. While they dared not think of themselves as indispensable to God's purposes, nor did they permit one another to evade the possibility that God could do something in and through them for the good of others.

Bill and Angie were hardly the first Methodists, then, to shake their heads in wonder at the improbability that they would be the persons who would take action that would turn out to be significant. Earlier generations of Methodist clergy and laity would have likely pointed to the role of Providence and the guiding presence of the Holy Spirit as theological explanations for how it is that ordinary people like Bill and Angie could find themselves in these situations. The fact that Angie had not even been named president of the student council until the week before the integration struggle took place would probably have evoked the memory of the Old Testament story of Esther, the young Hebrew women who found herself brought to the kingdom of Nebuchadnezzar "for such a time as this" to save her people.

55

Methodist clergy of earlier generations could also identify with the apostolic experience of St. Paul, who as he explained to the church at Corinth, saw his efforts coordinated by God's providential direction: "I planted, Apollos watered, but God gave the increase." (I Corinthians 3:6) Bill Wilder and his fellow clergy in the North Arkansas Conference would have taken seriously the fact that their individual efforts would have had to being construed collectively in order to account for whatever "moral progress" they might be making. Bill Wilder understood that Bob Sessions, the preceding pastor at St. John's Methodist Church, had also talked about the importance of "brotherhood" and racial reconciliation prior to Bill's arrival in 1956 to serve as pastor, and he tried to build on the efforts of his colleague. Although they tended to use modern idioms to convey their convictions in such matters, Sessions and Wilder were part of a generation that still recalled the early Wesleyan mission of "spreading scriptural holiness across the land and reforming the continent beginning with the church."

Beyond the ecclesial narratives that might be traced, there is the question of how the events described in this article fit into the life stories of Angie Evans and William M. Wilder. This is not the place to tell the life stories of these two people and their families or the ways their lives would unfold in the years to come. I would be remiss, however, if I did not observe that while others saw them as playing quasi-heroic roles, this was not their appraisal of what was going on. Both of them were aware of the fact that African American students and pastors and laypeople were also taking risks, exhibiting course, and exercising leadership. Neither of them had imagined that his or her actions would turn out to have such significance much less that they would receive accolades from near and far. Both felt awkward about how much attention and praise was heaped upon them as individuals in the months that followed the end of the Van Buren integration struggle.

In addition, Angie and Bill both had family concerns with which to contend in the fall of 1958. Angie's parents struggled with the fact that the actions their daughter had taken went beyond their own moral convictions about race, and they feared for her life in the midst of different kinds of threats that they received, from which they tried to shield her as much as possible. Bill Wilder and his wife Imo Jean also had other concerns that year. In September 1958, their four-year-old daughter

Pamela was receiving treatment for leukemia. Pam would die the following year. Instead of a time of moral victory, the 1958-59 school year would be remembered in the Wilder family as a wrenching time when Bill and Imo Jean cared for their beloved daughter as she suffered and ultimately died. In sum: Bill's involvement in the integration struggle was not even the primary focus of his family's concern at that time.[43]

All of which underlines the "improvised" character of the actions taken by Wilder and Evans in the context of the Van Buren integration struggle. The pastor and the teenager were by no means "ready" for the fact that they suddenly had this opportunity to offer a Christian witness. As Anglican theological ethicist Samuel Wells points out, Christians need not be embarrassed that their witness to the Kingdom of God is often improvised. On the contrary, the ability of Christian leaders to act results from their having been "schooled in a tradition so thoroughly that they learn to act from habit in ways appropriate to the circumstance."[44] Like previous generations, who struggled to discern the hand of providence in the events of human history, Bill and Angie marveled that the God who led the children of Israel out of the wilderness was the same God who was raising up leaders for the Kingdom.[45]

End Notes

1. See, for example, W. J. Cunningham's memoir of his experiences as pastor (1963-1966) of the congregation of Galloway Methodist Church in Jackson, Mississippi, *Agony at Galloway: Once Church's Struggle with Social Change* (Jackson: University Press of Mississippi, 1980).

2. See for example Clayborne Carson's discussion of the prophetic leadership given by the Reverend Mr. James Lawson, Jr., in his study of the Student Nonviolent Coordinating Committee *In Struggle: SNCC and the Black Awakening of the 1960s* (Cambridge, MA: Harvard University Press, 1981), pp. 19-30.

3. See for example, James F. Findlay, Jr., *Church People in the Struggle: The National Council of Churches and the Black Freedom Movement, 1950-1970* (New York: Oxford University Press, 1993).

4. 1948 *Book of Discipline of the Methodist Church*, Para. 2026, p. 601, see point #3.

5. Juan Williams, *Eyes on the Prize: America's Civil Rights Years: 1956-1965.* (New York, NY: Viking Penguin, 1988), p. 92.

6. Letter from William M. Wilder to Michael G. Cartwright, June 6, 1994.

7. For example, in the Report on World Peace of the 1948 *Journal of the North Arkansas Annual Conference*, item #4 indicated: "That all churches observe 'Brotherhood Week' and 'Race Relations Day'" (page 70).

8. See 1952 *Journal of the North Arkansas Conference* p. 32, third paragraph. A similar note appears in the 1953 Journal of the North Arkansas Conference, p. 22.

9. Lewis Howard Grimes, *A History of the Perkins School of Theology* (Dallas, Texas: Southern Methodist University Press, 1993), p. 158.

10. McDonald invited area churches to attend a concert of the (integrated) gospel choir made up of soldiers from Fort Chaffee, in nearby Barling, Arkansas.

11. The 1954 *Journal of the North Arkansas Conference*, Report of "Social and Economic Relations" committee, p. 23.

12. The two leaders most often mentioned as opposing the actions of Beal, McDonald and Wilder were Henry W. Goodloe and Sewell. B. Wilford. It is not known whether either or both were involved in "squelching" the report of the Board of Social and Economic Concerns.

13. Emphasis added. It is not clear what the sources of the internal quotations in this state-ment are. My attempts to clarify this question have not been successful.

14. The *New York Times*, September 5, 1958, p.16. Hereafter references to this source will be listed in abbreviated fashion as "NYT."

15. *Southwest Times/Southwest American*, September 8, 1958, p. 1. Hereafter references to this newspaper will be abbreviated as "SWT/A."

16. NYT, September 5, 1958, p.16.

17. According to Look magazine article of December 9, 1958, no one by this name was enrolled at the Van Buren Senior High School. Who was this person? Is there any particular significance to the name? Is this an intentional reference to Roger Williams, the early American Baptist dissenter? Or was this a matter of coincidence?

18. Associated Press report as carried in the NYT, Sept. 6, 1958, p. 16.

19. Ibid.

20. NYT, September 5, 1958, p.16; SWT/A, September 5, 1958, p. 1.

21. Ibid.

22. Letter of William M. Wilder to Michael G. Cartwright, June 8, 1994.

23. Ibid., p. 1.

24. NYT, Sept. 6, p. 6.

25. As best as I can ascertain, all of the African American leaders mentioned above were members of the Greater Pilgrim Baptist Church in Van Buren, whose pastor at that time was Rev. W. A. Wagner. There are no records of any involvement by members of Mt. Olive Methodist Church, the other African American Methodist Church in town, which at that time would have been part of the Southwest Conference of the Methodist Church (i.e., part of the Central Jurisdiction, the segregated structure created in 1939).
It is a poignant reminder of the determinative effects of the segregated structure of the Methodist Church, that William Wilder, the pastor of St. John's Methodist Church did not even know where Mt. Olive Methodist Church was located until much later, when he served as district superintendent of the Fort Smith district of the United Methodist Church.

26. NYT, Sept. 6, p. 6.

27. SWT/A, September 7, 1958, p. 1.

28. According to Wilder, who retained a copy of the typescript of sermon in question, the title was actually "Putting God First (A Communion Meditation)."

29. Wilder's sermon, which is imbued with several rhetorical appeals to the Israelite theocracy, is notable given the state motto of Arkansas: Regnat populi—"The people rule" which was often interpreted to mean that the "vox populi" the voice of the popular opinion should direct state government.

30. According to one account, approximately one-half of the students who had boycotted classes on Thursday and Friday of the previous week, returned to classes on Monday, which would suggest that support for the strike was weakening. However, according to other accounts, by this point in the struggle, approximately seventy-eight student strikers had been "expelled" (in the technical sense used by Superintendent Kelley) [see the later Look magazine article for example].

31. SWT/A, September 9, 1958.

32. Part of what made it plausible for these students to dare think that a majority of students at Van Buren High School might approve of integration is their awareness of the fact that there already were informal ties between black and white students who regularly played together in sandlot baseball games and other sports. Thus, there was probably more contact between the youth of the city of Van Buren at this time than there would have been between the adults.

33. As reported in *Newsweek*, September 22, 1958 and AP Wire Service report of September 11, 1958.

34. Ibid.

35. Ultimately, the NAACP's legal actions, which at an earlier point in the struggle received a great deal of local press coverage but which were almost invisible in national press accounts, were largely ineffectual. The NAACP filed a lawsuit against the local school board on Monday, September 22nd. Federal Judge John E. Miller denied the petition for an injunction against the school board, but retained jurisdiction in the case indefinitely while placing the school board and the wider community of Van Buren "on its honor" to resume integration of its public school system.

36. NYT, Tues. Sept. 23, 1958, p. 1. Renewed threats of a walkout by white students were not carried out. According to another news report, "There were only minor taunts and hard looks as the Negroes went to school for the first time in more than two weeks. Four Negro students eligible to return failed to appear. At the nearby junior high school, three of five enrolled Negroes returned to class without incident."

37. Immediately prior to William Wilder's appointment to St. John's Methodist Church, Robert Paul Sessions had been the pastor. Rev. Sessions, like Wilder, was an active proponent of integration within the North Arkansas Annual Conference during the late 1950s.

38. Patricia Carbine wrote the article about Angie Evans that was published in *Look*, p. 25.

39. Ibid.

40. One of the letters that she received was from the Goshen Mennonite Youth Fellowship in Goshen, Indiana, which among other things inquired about the similarities and differences between the two "M. Y. F." groups.

41. See "About Facts and Folks" section of *The Arkansas Methodist* newspaper, Dec. 4, 1958, page 8. It should be noted that neither William M. Wilder nor Angie Evans has any memory of this event having occurred. While there can be no question that North Arkansas conference officials intended to honor Ms. Evans, there is reason to believe that the Bible was never delivered to Ms. Evans.

42. See the letter of Philip B. Hodgson to Angie Evans.

43. Years later, Bill Wilder would write a letter to his youngest daughter, Elizabeth Riddle-Wilder, in which he would reflect on the role of God's providence in relation to the death of their daughter in 1959 while the family was living in Van Buren, Arkansas.

44. Samuel Wells, *Improvisation: The Drama of Christian Ethics* (Grand Rapids, MI: Brazos Press, 2004), 65.

45. An earlier version of this material was presented at the "Methodism and Missions Conference" of the North American Region of the World Methodist Historical Society Madison, NJ, August 13-16, 1994. Subsequently, in 1995, I revised and expanded the section of that paper that dealt with the Van Buren integration in a booklet that was privately produced and circulated to members of the Wilder family and selected friends and scholarly colleagues. Copies of *On Not Being Conformed to this World: Reflections on the Van Buren Integration Struggle and Its Aftermath 1958-1959* are available from the author.

Many persons have assisted me with the research for this paper, more than is usually the case in research projects of this kind:

First, my former research assistant at Allegheny College, Ms. Jennifer Smith, '97, cheerfully ran down "research leads" and shared my sense of delight in discovering tidbits from newspapers of this era. Jennifer was especially helpful in completing the archive file on Angela Evans Benham.

Ms. Angie Evans Benham, Ph.D., was gracious enough to let me have access to her personal archive from this era, and her nephew Richard Holmes did a wonderful job of collating and copying these materials for my use. My late father-in-law, the Reverend Mr. William M. Wilder (1923-2001), allowed me to have access to his personal files for letters and documents related to the Van Buren integration struggle.

Library and archival assistance from several different archival sources has enabled me to complete this project in a timely way. First, the staff of the Fort Smith Public Library, although initially reluctant, ultimately were very helpful in helping me to obtain copies of articles from the *Southwest Times Record/American* newspaper, the de facto "newspaper of record" for the 1958 Van Buren integration crisis by virtue of the fact that it was the only newspaper to cover the entire Van Buren integration struggle from start to finish. Second, Ms. Cynthia Burton, of the Pelletier Library at Allegheny College was extremely cooperative in arranging for me to have access to various materials from both of these libraries in Arkansas. As always, Cynthia was her cheerful self in the midst of dealing with my strange research requests. Third, Jane Dennis and her staff at *The Arkansas United Methodist* newspaper were very helpful in locating an article about Angie Evans that was published in the predecessor news organ for the two conferences of Arkansas Methodism.

Finally, I am very grateful to everyone who took the time to read an earlier, very rough, draft of this paper and offered comments and corrections: the Rev. Jim Beal, the Rev. Mary Wilder Cartwright, the Rev. Dr. L. Gregory Jones, the Rev. William M. Wilder, the Rev. Dr. C. Jarrett Gray, Jr. Each provided critical comments and corrections.

Leading Arkansas Methodists "Out of This Wilderness of Fear and Prejudice":

The Struggle for Racial Integration of Hendrix College, 1955-1965

Michael G. Cartwright

The story of how Hendrix College in Conway, Arkansas, came to be a racially integrated Methodist Church-related institution is a complex tale that involves many players—some African American and some Euro-American—including students, faculty, administration, alumni and trustees. I do not pretend that I am in a position to narrate all of the significant moments in the history of Hendrix College race relations,[1] much less to present a full chronicle of the struggle for racial integration. I have no doubt that other students of the history of Hendrix College are more competent to tell these stories. I do want, however, to tell the story of a series of events and actions that took place between 1955-1965 as a group of Hendrix administrators, faculty and trustees attempted to respond to the pleas of a small group of Arkansas Methodist clergy (most of whom were Hendrix alumni) who forthrightly made the moral case for integration at a time when most Arkansas Methodists did not support racial integration of public schools and private colleges.

What transpired at Hendrix after 1954 was by no means isolated from the Civil Rights struggle elsewhere in Arkansas. In a related article about the involvement of north Arkansas Methodists in the Civil Rights struggle, I have narrated the events that led up to the Van Buren integration struggle in September 1958 and the ways that Angie Evans, a fifteen-year-old student from St. John's Methodist Church, and her pastor, Reverend Bill Wilder, were surprised to discover themselves exercising leadership in support of Civil Rights for African Americans. Although that article focused on the struggle to integrate public schools at the local level, conversations about the prospect of racial integration in Methodist Church-related institutions in Arkansas were already in view. As early as 1955, North Arkansas Conference clergy leaders had called for Hendrix College to take action in this regard. By 1960, the Civil Rights struggle in Arkansas had shifted to private church-related colleges and universities where the struggle had a very different pattern of conflict.

As the focus of the struggle shifted, a different portrait of conflict came into view. By the fall of 1960, a small group of North Arkansas Conference clergy, which included Bill Wilder, Charles McDonald, Robert Paul Sessions, and Jim Beal, actively advocated the integration of Hendrix College. The focus of their attempts to persuade the faculty and administration of Hendrix to move toward racial integration was a cadre of fellow Methodists, some of whom were their former professors, fellow Methodist clergy, and laity who formed the board of trustees of the college. All of these moral actors were keenly aware that the support of Methodist congregations throughout the state of Arkansas would be critical to a successful resolution of this matter.

In the midst of contending with one another about how to move forward, these young clergymen found themselves bewildered and yearning for the kind of moral leadership that would enable Arkansas Methodism as a whole to make the transition from a world defined by racial segregation to a set of racially inclusive congregations. Looking for a Moses-like figure who could lead them out of "this wilderness of fear and prejudice," they acted within the limits of the moral authority that they shared as church leaders even as they attempted to use the structures of church governance to bring about the changes for which they called.

Unlike the Van Buren struggle, the integration of Hendrix College ultimately would come about not so much in response to the efforts of north Arkansas Methodist leaders like Bill Wilder, but because of changes in public policy that made segregation financially untenable for the college. In the end, the leadership that was able to effect the institutional change was more pragmatic than prophetic, and Methodist leaders at the college, as well as within the Annual Conference, would continue to wrestle with the recalcitrance of the majority of Euro-American Methodists in Arkansas, which preferred wandering in the wilderness to new political alignments in ecclesial and public spheres.

I. Background of the Struggle to Integrate Hendrix College: 1955-1961

The persuasive effort to bring about the integration of Hendrix College began more than five years earlier when Wilder and his colleagues decided to take action. The first time Hendrix College addressed the issue of integration was on October 18, 1955. The resolution asked Hendrix "to remove any bar or restriction to the admission of students because of race, creed, or religion." At Mr. Raney's suggestion, the resolution was referred to a committee that had just been authorized to study enrollment at the college.[2]

The next month, two resolutions had been passed "without dissenting vote" by the faculty on November 28, 1955.

1. We as Faculty members favor integration as the application of our Christian principles in human society.
2. We are ready to follow *the leadership of our Church* in working out the problem of integration as it relates to Hendrix College. (emphasis added)[3]

These faculty resolutions were presented at the first meeting of a "joint committee on integration representing the Hendrix College faculty and board of trustees" held at Hendrix on January 3, 1956.[4] In retrospect, it may or may not be significant that a dean of the college offered an exegesis of what "leadership of the church" in this instance meant to the Hendrix faculty. As he stated in a report to the board of trustees, "leadership of the church" constituted "*any actions that would be taken relative to integration at the Methodist General Conference in April-May 1956 and by the two Arkansas Annual Conferences.*" It is not immediately clear who first articulated this particular definition of "leadership," but clearly Hendrix College administrators were seeking some kind of *formal* authorization and/or mandate for action from the two Methodist conferences in Arkansas, as distinct from informal support that had been and would continue to be proffered from some of the conference's clergy.

The "joint committee" had a "free and informal discussion of integration and Hendrix, with no sharp difference of opinion being expressed." A member of the committee dutifully reported: "No attempt was made to formulate a statement of group opinion." The only action that was taken was to appoint a sub-committee, which would hold *additional* meetings, and report back to the committee prior to the April 1956 board meeting. One of the trustees appointed to that sub-committee was Aubrey G. Walton, a one-time member of the North Arkansas Conference and, at that time, pastor of First Methodist Church in Little Rock. According to notes from the sub-committee's first meeting, a member said, "the Church will be one of the last institutions to integrate, but has fought for it through literature, etc."

Subsequent to the October meeting, Hendrix faculty members were polled (in "executive session") in an attempt to give the board of trustees some sense of whether the faculty would "assist" integration or "resist" it. The form of the "Questionnaire on Integration" is noteworthy. Two assumptions were proposed for the faculty's consideration, both of which hinged on *actions to be taken* by the conferences of the Methodist Church. The first assumption stated:

> Assume that by July 1, 1956, the Methodist General Conference and the two Arkansas Annual Conferences have approved in general the principle of integration, and that the Hendrix Board of Trustees has asked the faculty to make a recommendation on the policy for Hendrix. Please check the statement which indicates how now you think you would vote: (Dec. 14, 1955).
> 1. To admit Negroes on the same basis and with the same privileges as other students in September, 1956.
> 2. To admit Negroes, on the same basis and with the same privileges as other students, at some later date.
> 3. To continue in the foreseeable future not admitting Negroes.
> 4 To admit Negroes, subject to any qualifications indicated below, in September 1956.
> 5. To admit Negroes, subject to any qualifications indicated below, at some later date.

Assumption #2 of the questionnaire stated: "Assume that the 1956 General Conference and the 1956 Arkansas Annual Conferences take no definitive action on integration and that the board of trustees asks the faculty for its recommendation. How would you answer the items above." As these two assumptions make clear, Hendrix officials were seeking clear evidence of "leadership," in the form of consensus from Arkansas Methodist conferences.

The results of this poll are informative. At one level, the results of the poll validated President Ellis' concern that the Hendrix faculty members were significantly *more supportive* of integration under the first assumption than they were in response to Assumption #2. Under Assumption #1, thirteen of thirty-five respondents favored "unrestricted admission," but under the second assumption *only eight* out of thirty-five favored unrestricted admission. Tellingly, the number of persons favoring "no admission in the foreseeable future" rose from five under Assumption #1 to eleven out of thirty-five respondents under Assumption #2. The only other significant change occurred in question #3 where seven respondents favored "unrestricted admission at a later date" under Assumption #1 but *only three* persons favored that proposal under Assumption #2.[5] Clearly, although a significant number of Hendrix faculty supported integration of the college, they were not going to pursue a change of policy without a significant mandate for change from the two Methodist Conferences in Arkansas in relation to the actions of the General Conference of the Methodist Church.

Several related factors also played a role in the hesitation of officials at Hendrix College to pursue racial integration. First, during the mid-to-late 1950s, student enrollment at Hendrix *declined* at a time when other private colleges and public universities in Arkansas were experiencing an increase in enrollment. Second, during this same period Hendrix began to pursue a strategy of academic excellence, seeking to become more academically selective in its admissions. Third, recruitment of women also increased as the college built more residence halls to house women students. In sum, during the six-year period between 1955 and 1961, Hendrix administrators faced several strategic challenges all at the same time.

II. North Arkansas Methodists Seeking New Leadership for the Struggle: 1960-61

All of the actions taken by North Arkansas Conference committees (see the chapter in this volume regarding Van Buren High School) and Hendrix College faculty were in view when, in the spring of 1960, the board of trustees voted *not* to integrate Hendrix College. By this time, the North Arkansas Conference's discussion of this matter had been going on for at least six years. As Rev. Sessions recalled in a letter addressed to Hendrix President Marshall T. Steel, "on June 19, 1954, the North Arkansas Annual Conference adopted a report (by a standing vote), by its Board of Social and Economic Relations welcoming the Supreme Court decision on integration as "*a reflection of the Christian ideal,' and calling on our people to pray and work 'with varying timeliness' for the achievement of that ideal in all areas of life, including the institutions of the church.*" (emphasis added).[6]

Given the concerns about "leadership" articulated by the Hendrix faculty and administration, it is worth noting that the board of trustees ultimately took action on the question of integration in response to an *unofficial request* by a group of young ministers in the North Arkansas Annual Conference. In May 1959, Robert Paul Sessions addressed a letter to Mr. George E. Pike, of Dewitt, Arkansas, the president of the Board of Trustees at Hendrix College. In that letter, Sessions, writing on behalf of himself "and a group of interested members of the North Arkansas Annual Conference," asked Pike to present their petition to the board of trustees at their May 5, 1959, meeting. Sessions made clear that the purpose of the letter was twofold:

> We write because of a concern for the spiritual and material progress of Hendrix. It is our understanding that Dr. Steel will present to the board at this time other ideas and dreams concerning Hendrix. We firmly believe that an admissions policy in keeping with the highest ideals of the Methodist Church and of our Christian faith will be a big step toward making Hendrix all that God would have it be.

In one sense, Sessions and his colleagues were clearly acting unofficially, without the explicit authorization of the North Arkansas Annual Conference, but at the same time, his letter was informed by a series of previous actions taken by boards and committees of the Annual Conferences over the preceding five years.

In fact, Sessions' letter carefully documented the series of actions taken by the North Arkansas Annual Conference as well as called attention to the fact that as of May 1959, "the College of the Ozarks, all our state colleges, and (even earlier) the University of Arkansas, have announced admissions policies based on individual qualifications rather than race, with a minimum of public opposition and little if any adverse effect on their enrollments." Sessions' letter concluded with the following plea for action:

Since the aim of Hendrix is to be a Christian college in every way possible, and since our General Conference and Arkansas Annual Conferences repeatedly have stated that discrimination because of race is unChristian, and since other colleges in the state have led the way and shown that an open admissions policy is practical on the college-level in Arkansas, we therefore ask you, the trustees of Hendrix, to adopt, at your meeting May 5, 1959, a policy of admitting qualified applicants regardless of their race or national origin. If you should vote otherwise, we would appreciate knowing:
(a) What action has been taken,
(b) Whether the majority of the board agrees with last year's North Arkansas Conference that "removing barriers of discrimination is … ethically and morally right," and
(c) When the board believes the racial barriers at Hendrix can be removed.

Contrary to Bob Sessions' wishes, the board of trustees did not act on this matter in 1959. However, on March 29, 1960, the trustees did take up the question, and the result was not what Sessions wanted to hear. The press release provided by the public relations department of Hendrix College was unambiguous: "The Hendrix College Board of Trustees voted today to continue the College's long-standing policy of accepting white students only." The full statement of the board made it clear that the trustees were not willing to take the lead when it was apparent that the majority of Methodist laity in Arkansas was *against* racial integration of church congregations and institutions:

The Trustees of Hendrix College have been asked by certain individuals and groups to consider the advisability of integrating the College at an early date.

The matter was referred to the executive board of the board of trustees last spring. Members of the executive committee have discussed the matter together. They have also discussed it individually with many leaders of the church in Arkansas, both laymen and ministers.

We are convinced that the majority of the Methodist people in the state do not want any change in the admission policy of the college. We, therefore, register our support of the present policy for the admission of students.

The College is grateful for the privilege of serving the Methodist Church in Arkansas. The trustees will always try to understand and to serve the Methodist Churches in Arkansas who have entrusted this institution to our care.

As this statement indicates, the Hendrix trustees were acutely aware of *how limited* the support for integration was among Methodists in the state of Arkansas. However committed Sessions and his colleagues were to the policy of integration, they simply did not have a basis of support among the congregations of their own conference. Also, as the aforementioned account of the suppression of the report of the Committee on Social and Economic Concerns suggests, there continued to be some resistance on the part of the clergy leadership of the conference as well. In fact, some of the very members of the Hendrix board of trustees who voted against integration in March of 1960 were clergy members in the North Arkansas Conference of the Methodist Church. Aubrey Walton and Arthur Terry, trustees from the Little Rock Conference *opposed* integration at that time; the Reverend Fred Roebuck, a North Arkansas Conference trustee, was undecided. The only minister representing the two conferences of Arkansas Methodism on the Hendrix board of trustees who was unambiguously in favor of integration of Hendrix in 1960 was A. W. Martin, Sr.

The press release issued by the college following the board of trustees meeting provided a second reason in justification of the trustees' action. Bishop Paul E. Martin offered the assurance that "Today's action does not mean that the Methodist Church is ignoring the educational needs of Negroes." Martin called attention to Philander Smith College in Little Rock, another Methodist Church-related institution which was also accredited by the North Central Association of Colleges and Universities. Martin's comments, which called attention to the historically black college that served pastors and congregations in the Central Jurisdiction of the Methodist Church, actually served to underscore the Methodist Church's own segregated structure at this time. Hendrix officials would later note that some on the board of trustees had expressed concern that "taking black students would weaken Philander Smith. It would be competition with Philander Smith."[7]

News of the board of trustees' action elicited a round of correspondence between officials at Hendrix and ministers of the North Arkansas Conference of the Methodist Church. William M. Wilder, at that time pastor of First Methodist Church in Heber Springs, articulated the views of other Methodist ministers who responded to the news with great anger. Wilder minced no words in conveying to Dr. Marshall T. Steel his anger about the board's decision.

I was sickened as I read in the [*Arkansas*] *Gazette* of the decision of the Hendrix Trustees concerning segregation, and of your concurrence in that decision. Perhaps the most unfortunate part of this decision is that it places our church in the untenable position of accepting the desires of people, rather than holding up the standards of Christian brotherhood and the Methodist *Book of Discipline*....

As a minister in The Methodist Church, I feel betrayed by your action. The effectiveness of what I, or any other local pastor, may have to say on Christian brotherhood as it applies to race relations is pretty well destroyed by leadership in high places which blandly assumes that we must go along with the crowd.[8]

Wilder's concern for the integrity of Methodist disciplinary practice notwithstanding, there is some reason to believe that the members of the board of trustees were more concerned about slippage between what North Arkansas Methodists were and were not saying in official actions and what was actually taking place in the typical Methodist congregation in Arkansas. A. W. Martin, director of the Wesley Foundation at the University of Arkansas at Fayetteville, and a Hendrix Trustee, articulated the problem this way in his letter to Charles McDonald.

In general, we might as well face it, we have a terrific job [to do] in educating our people along the lines that moral principles are really involved in segregation. Until this issue can be faced on the basis of *what is right* there is little hope of resolving it in terms of Christian principles. As long as we confuse the right to one's opinion with the assumption that the right *to* an opinion is identical with a *right opinion*, we are due for a lot of trouble. Instead, there must be insistence that all our opinions must be submitted to higher authority; namely God himself.[9]

At the same time, Martin himself observed that the trustees' decision had little moral integrity.

Interestingly enough no one so much as suggested that what they were doing was *right*. The sole argument advanced in support of the board action was that "this is what the majority of Methodist people in Arkansas want."

In the background there seems to be a paralyzing fear that grips the minds and hearts of Methodist leaders in Arkansas—a fear that things will be disturbed and changed....

Right now, the administration at Hendrix and a majority of the board believe that the way to success, student enrollment and financial wise, is along the segregation road. "For white students only " is to be the basis of our appeal. And the results thus far appear to support the wisdom of this decision.

It has been quite some time since I have heard any expression of concern on the part of responsible leaders in the Methodist Church in Arkansas for the role that a church-related college should play in clarifying and practicing the principles and procedures that presumably might lead our people out of this wilderness of fear and prejudice. March 29 will, in my opinion, be remembered as a dark day in the life of Hendrix and of Arkansas Methodism. The far-reaching implications of the board's action are staggering.[10]

Martin's commentary is significant for several reasons. First, it calls attention to the apparent *absence* of "responsible leadership" on the part of north Arkansas Methodists regarding the role of Hendrix College in leading God's people "out of the wilderness" of racism. On the one hand this suggests a lack of imaginative leadership on the part of the Methodist Church in Arkansas; on the other hand, it reveals a significant set of moral expectations is now being thrust on Hendrix College by church leaders. Significantly, in his perceptive set of remarks, the Rev. A. W. Martin assumes the congruence of the college's mission with that of the church. Here it is possible to discern a subtle but important shift in perspectives: *whereas in 1956 college officials were looking to the Methodist Church for leadership, now church officials are looking to the college for leadership.*

The issue of integration was discussed again at the North Arkansas Annual Conference meeting at Mt. Sequoyah in June 1960. Once again, a resolution was prepared and readied for presentation on the Annual Conference floor. Once again, many participants felt that "the administration of the College should be contacted *before* the resolution was presented. Dr. Marshall Steel met with this group of (primarily younger) ministers who were urging the college to integrate.[11] Significantly, Dr. Steel did not attempt to persuade the group to refrain from presenting the resolution to the Annual Conference. Nor did he give any clear indication about *what he would do* in response to their urging, although this should not be taken to mean that Steel was himself in any sense opposed to integration.[12] However, he did suggest that an appearance before the college's board of trustees might serve a better purpose for all concerned. In the end, the group acceded to Steel's redirection of their proposed action.

Accordingly, in 1961 at the spring meeting of the Board of Trustees of Hendrix College, a group of three Methodist ministers, Jim Beal, Charles McDonald and William M. Wilder, presented a statement to the board on behalf of a larger group of Methodist ministers. Their opening statement makes clear their concern not to alienate officials at the institution that also happened to be their alma mater. However, the net effect of their presentation was to attempt to persuade the board to reverse its decision of the previous spring.

> We do not want to be misunderstood as to our purpose for being here. Simply and honestly, we are here because we love and appreciate Hendrix College and are interested in its future. We are pleased with the remarkable physical progress the college is making, and, yet, certain things cause us concern. We refer specifically to the statement and press release by the trustees last spring relative to the admission policy of the College. We do not mean to pass judgment on you for this action; rather, we confess our sin and failure that this decision was reached. We realize that we must bear the blame in the matter because the board's actions clearly illustrates that our witness for Christ to the Methodists of Arkansas in the area of Brotherhood has not been what it should have been. We ask the forgiveness of God for the lack of Christian witness in the area of Brotherhood.

After explaining the sequence of events that had led them to this meeting, Beal and his colleagues assured the trustees that "it was agreed that no publicity would be given the matter either before or after the meeting with the board."

> We are here to request that the part of the admission policy related to a man's race be left an open question. We observe that the college has no *written* policy of admission which separates persons according to race; this part of the admission policy is one of tradition, not of record. We earnestly hope, then, that the board's decision to "continue the present admission policy" might be construed to mean the admission of any qualified student. The entrance requirements, relative to academic standards and character traits, to our college are high, and that is as it should be. The high quality of work of Hendrix students would not be lowered, we feel, if the board agreed to admit any qualified student; too many other things are operative besides of color of a man's skin. Our sincere desire is that we may be able to continue to discuss this matter as an open, not a closed, matter.

The ministers proceeded to call attention to Hendrix College's relationship with the Methodist Church, observing that, among other things, "The church is a connectional institution which includes the colleges, and the college has the responsibility and the right to lead the church in many areas, even as it has done in the past." Here several examples are offered, ranging from providing academic freedom for teachers who taught unpopular views (higher criticism of the Bible, evolution, etc.) to encouraging "social dancing" in the face of disapproval of many north Arkansas Methodists, and the college's recent display of courage in withdrawing from intercollegiate football.

After praising Hendrix's many examples of intellectual and moral leadership in the past, Beal turned to the reasoning given by the board for not integrating Hendrix.

> The board's report last spring indicated that the admission policy action was taken because it was felt that this expressed the wishes of the majority of Methodists in Arkansas. This may or may not be, and yet, many of us hoped to see the board take a position of responsible leadership in this important area of human relations, even as the College has led in other areas.

After invoking the notion of "responsible leadership," the delegation of ministers from the North Arkansas Annual Conference turned its attention to the task of making the case for why the board of trustees should reverse itself.

Among the reasons offered, McDonald called attention to the theological dimension of ethics: "There is the uncompromising Christian ethic which implies that love for God means love for man, all men; ..." Later in this same document, the ministers specified the biblical basis for the Christian ethic of inclusiveness: "The New Testament teaches us that Christ came to break down the middle wall which divides people. We hope that we all can feel that this is a part of our *mission* in the world."

Beal then shifted from the theological mandate for the church's mission to what was already happening in the world, calling the board's attention to the fact that all public colleges and universities had already adopted a policy of "open admission" regarding race. They also reminded the trustees of the series of resolutions by the Board of Social and Economic Concerns and the Board of Education (see above) calling for integration of church institutions, including the 1955 Board of

Education resolution which called for the college to "remove any bar or restriction to the admission of students because of race, creed, or religion." However, Beal and his colleagues were keenly aware that any kind of moral argument that the North Arkansas Conference might offer would be severely weakened by the widespread pattern of segregation in the Methodist congregations of north Arkansas. "We must confess that few of the Methodist churches in Arkansas have Negroes as members or as worshippers; there are some. Many of us are concerned about this, and are working for the time when any seeking, sincere, person can worship in our churches, or, rather, Christ's church."

They concluded their list of counter-arguments by calling attention to the changing world situation, and the place of Methodists in that world.

> Another factor which would seem to favor a different action is the world situation in which we live. For the purely selfish reason of preservation of our country and ourselves, we are going to have to rethink our attitudes toward other people. We are in the spotlight whether we wish it so or not. Our African and Asian brothers are looking to us as the witnesses of Jesus Christ, and too often we disappoint them. The witness of such missionaries as Jon Guthrie, a graduate of Hendrix now serving in Elizabethville, Republic of Congo, [Katanga, Africa] is hampered by action of this Board. Of course, it isn't just this action. It's the whole image of America in this area of Brotherhood. These things would seem to say that the matter before us is one we must keep open for discussion.

The moral appeal of this statement was strong for those *already disposed to agree* with the ministers. But in this instance, what was more persuasive to the board of trustees was the fact that the vast majority of Methodists in north Arkansas *disagreed* with these ministers. Even more poignant was the implicit recognition—by both the ministers and the college officials—that the local churches would be among *the last* institutions in the state of Arkansas to integrate,[13] a fact that severely undercut the prophetic appeal of Beal and his colleagues.

III. Marshall T. Steel's Leadership and the Integration of Hendrix College: 1961-1965

The attempt by this group of younger Methodist clergy to give leadership in the midst of complex considerations did not succeed, at least not in ways that they would have found satisfactory. The board of trustees did not act as they requested, and integration at Hendrix did not take place *in direct response* to the efforts of north Arkansas Methodist clergy leaders. What *did* happen was that after this meeting in the Spring of 1961, the president of Hendrix College, Marshall T. Steel, began to move in more deliberate ways to lay the groundwork for the racial integration of the college. However, ultimately, *the way* that Steel maneuvered did not attempt to address the concern raised by Trustee A. W. Martin, Sr., i.e., how Hendrix College could go about leading Arkansas Methodists "out of this wilderness of fear and prejudice." The reason why has everything to do with the way the church-college relationship was altered within the context of the decision to integrate, a decision which finally came about principally because of Marshall T. Steel's leadership.

It is beyond the scope of this paper to provide a full account of President Marshall T. Steel's life. Most observers would agree that he was a complex man. A four-time delegate to General Conference and pastor for twenty-two years (1936-1958) at Highland Park Methodist Church in Dallas, Texas, Steel came to Hendrix at a time of heightened expectations, declining enrollment, and a long list of needs. By employing a highly centralized corporate administrative style in contrast to the more democratic style of administration of his predecessor, Steel succeeded in making many good things happen at Hendrix College during his tenure as president (1958-1969).

However, in his zeal for the present and the future, Steel often disregarded the past, and in the process, significant changes occurred without being acknowledged as such. As James E. Lester, Jr., put it so well, in retrospect, Marshall T. Steel was the "catalyst" for what was clearly "a transitional era" in the history of Hendrix College.[14] All of this gives a background to the way Steel dealt with the delegation of young Methodist ministers who attempted to intervene in 1960-1961 to get the board of trustees to authorize integration at Hendrix. Clearly, while Steel recognized the significance of their collective initiative, he did not recognize these ministers as *authorized* by the Conference to exercise leadership in this regard. However much they might be acting in the best interests of the conference and the college, he remarked in an oral history interview in 1979,

> [T]hey didn't represent the [Methodist] church. They represented themselves, and maybe they represented people that I didn't know about. I'm sure that I did not like the idea of their coming to the board and going over my head with recommendations to it. I'm sure I told them not to do it that way.

As Steel made clear in his assessment of the events of spring 1961, he had a different conception of what leadership involved.

> A lot of things that I had to deal with [as president of Hendrix], I had to deal with by talking to people confidentially and building their confidence and going about what I thought was leadership; whereas if I had to deal with a reporter, and he blasted me in the paper, I could get more opposition generated before I could get the work done. And I felt these young fellows were adding to my problem. I was working on the matter. I wasn't working as fast as they wanted it....

Steel's comments may also shed some light on his own actions as president of Hendrix College. In March 1960, Steel appears to have been primarily concerned about the possible backlash evoked by an announcement that Hendrix trustees had voted to integrate the college in a circumstance in which there was clearly no consensus among Arkansas Methodists to pursue integration. Accordingly, he cautioned the board about the consequences of integrating Hendrix *at that particular time*.[15] However, this lack of consensus among Methodist clergy and laity of the North Arkansas Conference *did not prevent* Steel from attempting to "get the job done" in his own way. Accordingly, over the next three years, Steel carefully maneuvered—always in close consultation with the board of trustees—to "set the stage" for eventual integration of the college.

The official minutes of the meetings of the board of trustees from 1962 to 1964 display President Steel's deliberate, if demonstrably pragmatic, leadership at work. First, in the spring of 1962, after having reminded the board of trustees of the visit by the delegation of ministers the year before, Steel established an exchange student program between Hendrix College and Philander Smith College. This new relationship was the basis for policy changes in the dining halls at Hendrix College, a decision for which he took responsibility, calling it "an administrative matter" about which he officially informed the board of trustees after the fact.[16] In retrospect, this was *the first real step* in the desegregation of Hendrix College.

Then, in March 1963, Steel presented a report to the board of trustees, in which he carefully laid the groundwork for racial integration at the college, for reasons that had nothing to do with the arguments presented by the delegation of north Arkansas ministers two years before. The first part of Steel's report focused on significant shifts in the financial picture for the college (the ratio of student tuition to total costs of a Hendrix education, faculty salaries, student-faculty ratio, number of majors, etc). With these factors in mind, Steel called to the attention of the board "a problem related to building of a new dormitory."[17]

> At the last meeting of the board of trustees, you authorized the administration to apply for a loan from the federal government for the financing of our dormitory construction. Though you may not have thought of it in specific terms, since that action, President Kennedy has issued his order concerning integration in all projects financed by the federal government. We have recently learned that it will be necessary for the College to sign a statement to the effect that there will be no segregation in any new facilities financed by the federal government. At the present time this does not affect schools which are not integrated. However, it is the judgment of a great many people who are in a position to know, that within a relatively short time there will be either a presidential or a court order indicating that this commitment will involve us in the integration of the college. I am advised that the government is sure to hold to this basic principle; namely, that segregation at entrance to the college is in fact segregation in the dormitory.

In effect, Steel had *re-introduced* the question of integration, but it is significant to notice that he did so within the context of a larger set of issues: the college's ongoing struggle to improve its outdated residential facilities, and in particular, the concern to build another new residential hall for women in the midst of financial challenges (an issue that had been before the board of trustees when the issue of integration had first been broached nearly a decade before). As Steel goes on to suggest:

> You would be interested in knowing that the finance committee has discussed the possibilities of other methods of financing a loan for our dormitory. We are of the opinion that the Methodist Church is and will be taking rapid steps which would lead us to integration entirely unrelated to a federal loan. Inasmuch as we would apparently be moving toward integration in a relatively short time anyhow, it is the judgment of the finance committee that we should proceed to finance our dormitories with federal funds. I feel that the board should take time

to discuss this matter fully. If there are questions they should be brought clearly into the open. There must be no misunderstanding between us about the direction in which we are moving. It is our recommendation that we proceed with federal financing of our dormitories and our dining facilities. It is also our recommendation that the administration proceed in preparing groups intimately related to the College for all the problems related thereto.

Steel's comments about The Methodist Church in the preceding paragraph are difficult to assess. Strictly speaking, *nothing* in the policies of The Methodist Church *had changed* since the visit of the three ministers in 1961. The arguments that had been made on that occasion were no more (and no less!) persuasive now than they had been at that time. The only new thing that had changed was in the sphere of public policy, where the advent of new guidelines for federal loans to private colleges was placing pressure on institutions like Hendrix College to conform to the new conception of Civil Rights.

Even with this secular argument in view, the board of trustees was not yet ready to move on the matter,[18] but President Steel had provided recalcitrant trustees, like Methodist layman DuVall Perkins, with the kind of excuse he felt that he needed to take back home to explain to his friends and associates about why the Hendrix trustees would have to vote for integration within the next year. One year later, in March of 1964, Steel came back to the board of trustees with another proposal. As the minutes of the board of trustees demonstrate, Steel had spent much of the past year preparing the college and its constituencies for what was about to take place.

> Dr. Steel reported to the board that he had continued to study matters related to the integration of the College. He has had conferences with student groups, faculty, business leaders, church groups, and others in an effort to explain the situation which the College is facing and to give persons an opportunity to express their points of view on the matter. He indicated he had not asked any group to go on record with a vote, either for or against the proposals. He indicated his awareness that there are still many problems in front of us, but he said that he felt the time was at hand for the board of trustees to act on the matter.

At the conclusion of Steel's presentation, the Board of Trustees of Hendrix College passed a resolution that Steel proposed (upon a motion made by Dr. A. W. Martin, Sr., and seconded by Dr. Roebuck, the two ministerial members nominated by the North Arkansas Conference of the Methodist Church). The effect authorized "the faculty committee on admissions to admit qualified students" to the college. Although the change was subtle, it was significant.[19]

With trustee approval finally granted, and faculty authority in the matter of admissions reaffirmed, the college proceeded with integration, and in the fall semester of 1965, two African American women, Linda Pondexter of Hope and Emily Johnson of Little Rock, enrolled at Hendrix College.[20] Four years later, in the spring of 1969, Linda Pondexter was the first African American to graduate from Hendrix. Interestingly enough, the college's catalogue would not fully reflect the change in admissions policy until 1970-71, thereby officially advertising a policy that, *de facto*, had been in effect for nearly five years.[21] It would not be until later in the 1970s that more than a few African American students attended Hendrix each year. As all of these developments suggest, "the racial integration of Hendrix College was far from a pioneering effort at social change."[22]

As James E. Lester observed in his *Centennial History of Hendrix*, the college "changed its admissions policy for a variety of reasons." However, it is significant to observe that Lester's list of reasons for the change *does not include* the ongoing effort by north Arkansas Methodist pastors to get the trustees to relent. In point of fact, north Arkansas Methodist clergy leaders *did not succeed* in their effort to persuade the college, on moral and theological grounds, to integrate the college. The stratagem by which Marshal T. Steel *did succeed* in leading the Hendrix College Board of trustees to agree to allow integration to occur, in order to obtain federal funds to build another women's dormitory, while effective in the short run, has had unforeseen consequences.

While Steel's leadership in this matter has benefited the college in a variety of ways, it did not address the lingering question of who would lead Arkansas Methodists "out of this wilderness of fear and prejudice." But Marshall Steel might have argued that it is not "the task" of Hendrix College to lead Arkansas Methodists "out of the wilderness." That is the church's mission. But, that in turn raises the question of *the basis* of the church-college relationship if there is no longer a clearly discernible "shared" mission. In retrospect, the decision of the trustees appears to have also signaled an important shift in the church-college relationship.

But if such a shift did occur, it was probably even earlier than the decisions of 1963-64, and several factors suggest that this is the more apt conclusion. First, as I have already suggested, between 1956 and 1960 a discernible shift had already occurred between the church and the college in *who was looking to whom* for leadership. In 1956, the faculty of the college clearly was looking to the two Arkansas conferences for "the leadership of the church" (to use the words of the 1955 faculty resolution). This language suggested that the Hendrix faculty still saw themselves as sharing the Christian mission of the Methodist Church. Five years later, in 1961, a group of younger ministers appealed to the trustees of Hendrix College to offer "responsible leadership" to the Methodist Church, under the assumption that there was a mission that both bodies shared.

Second, assuming that the Hendrix faculty decisions in 1955 were made in good faith—and I see no evidence to the contrary—it would appear that under President Matt Ellis' administration, the faculty *did not believe* that it was its prerogative to set standards for admission. However, Marshall T. Steel's presentation to the board of trustees in 1964 clearly assumes that the faculty *did* have that prerogative (as defined in the Charter and By-Laws). While there is no question that in 1956 the Hendrix faculty was being realistic about the need for the concurrence of the board of trustees (and Arkansas Methodists) before proceeding toward integration, Marshall Steel's apparent re-interpretation of the rules of governance of the college (without acknowledgment) was unrealistic in its pretense that nothing had changed.[23]

In retrospect, there is reason to believe that Steel's candor with the trustees about the "real change" that was about to take place in the admissions policies of the college was not matched by candor with north Arkansas Methodist church leaders about a subtle but real change in the church-college relationship. To give him the benefit of the doubt, some might argue that Marshall Steel himself did not realize that such a change had occurred. However, circumstantial evidence makes this a difficult conclusion to sustain.[24] Moreover, the total pattern of Steel's dealings before the board of trustees, and his strategic use of procedural rules to get the board to agree to integration reflects the emergence of what might be called a new understanding of the church-college relationship, but one that was *not* the product of renegotiation on the part of both parties. Rather, in practice, Steel can be seen to have introduced a functional distinction in the church-college relationship in the context of his effort to bring about integration at Hendrix College.

Thus, one of *the most significant reasons why* the appeal of north Arkansas Methodist clergy leaders failed in their effort to integrate Hendrix College comes more clearly into view. When the delegation of north Arkansas clergy presented their case before the board of trustees, Beal, McDonald and Wilder were making their appeal under the assumption that the college and the conference "shared" a mission, which in turn made plausible their moral appeal to a social ethic based on the Christian vision of the "new humanity" (Ephesians 2:15) creat-ed where walls had been broken down; a vision which, they argued, is to be embodied in all aspects of the life of the church.

By contrast, Marshall Steel was much more comfortable with what might be called a *pragmatist* conception of church-college relations, in which the missions of the church and college are separated from one another *as different functions* within an "intangible" relationship. This does not mean that Marshall Steel himself did not share the moral per-spective of the clergy, but he did not regard their arguments, strictly speaking, as *applicable* to the college's policies and procedures. For him, *another set of values was operative* where the college was concerned. As he would later say,

> I want the college to be a church-related institution. I want it to be an institution the church can be proud of. I don't think it has to be a mission trying to do on the campus evangelistic work that the church might do at various times during the year. When you look at the actu-al operation, this has its problems.... I'm much more interested in an *intangible...* relationship where between the college and the church there is a feeling of mutual good will... even though I don't think the college's task is the same as the church's mission...

Steel's functionalist (utilitarian) distinction between the church's mission (i.e., evangelism) and the college's educational task, when taken on face value, is quite attractive until we confront the fact that an "intangible relationship" based on "a feeling of good will" is quite unsta-ble except where anchored in a clear understanding of what is and is not shared at the level of ethical commitments. And that is exactly what was lost in the struggle to integrate Hendrix College. The resulting pattern of "separate, but equal" missions for the church and the college was the clear, if unintended (and sadly ironic), outcome of the struggle to integrate Hendrix College during the decade from 1955 to 1965.[25]

IV. The Aftermath of the Struggle to Integrate Hendrix College

For all practical purposes, with the integration of Hendrix College in the fall of 1965, north Arkansas Methodist involvement in the integration struggle came to an end. While there would be other problems to confront, and the Board of Education and the Board of Economic and Social Concerns would continue to monitor progress of institutions related to the North Arkansas Conference,[26] the question of *institutional* integration had been resolved. However, as this paper demonstrates, one of the most significant problems disclosed by the integration struggle in Arkansas, and the participation of north Arkansas Methodist clergy and laity in it, was the perceived *crisis* of leadership. In this final section, I will attempt to shed some light on this crisis, first, by putting it into the context of the changes that unfolded after the integration of Hendrix College, and second, by calling attention to the existence of untold stories about Arkansas Methodists and Hendrix College.

A. Shifting Conceptions of Leadership: In retrospect, it may be significant that it was *not* the head of the school board in Van Buren who led the way in the integration struggle in September 1958, but a fifteen-year-old young woman whose "improvised" Christian witness caught everyone, including herself, off guard.[27] Angie Evans symbolizes the multiple shifts in leadership that were beginning to unfold. At this time, new leadership also emerged within the North Arkansas Conference in the face of the recalcitrance of a few prominent segregationist leaders in the conference. That young leaders like Sessions, Beal, McDonald, and Wilder were *not able* to persuade the Hendrix College Board of Trustees to integrate in 1960 stands as a reminder not only of the complexity of the times, but also of the complex "connectional" relationships that were being restructured in the Methodist Church in this era.[28] In short, the decade of 1955-1965 ushered in a time of change, including some very significant *changes in leadership* in the Methodist Church.

The leadership of *the Methodist Church as a denomination* would change: In some cases, these changes would represent significant gains, particularly in the structures and offices of the denomination. For example, within just a few years, the proposal for a "United Methodist Church," in which the (segregated) Central Jurisdiction was to be eliminated, would come to the floor of the North Arkansas Conference for approval, and the conference would have to confront the patterns of segregation within its own house. African Americans would be elected to serve as bishops and lead conferences comprised of predominantly Euro-American congregations. In other ways, the total pattern of changes would produce losses. During this time, many Methodists left the church, and Angie Evans would be among that company of younger leaders that The United Methodist Church lost to other denominations during the next two decades.[29]

The leadership of the *North Arkansas Conference* would change: During the Civil Rights era, younger ministers such as Beal, McDonald, and Wilder thought of themselves as opposing "the establishment,"[30] but over the next three decades, each of these ministers would each serve in the conference as district superintendents, with all three serving for two separate terms. To paraphrase Jim Beal: One day they all woke up to discover that they had *become* "the establishment" and others were challenging their conception of themselves as agents of social change in the conference.

The leadership *of Hendrix College* would change: In 1965, a new dean would be hired at Hendrix. Dr. Francis Christie led the faculty as they restructured the curriculum. Four years later, Marshall T. Steel would retire—the *last* Methodist clergyman[31] to serve as president of Hendrix College. Thereafter, lay United Methodists would serve as the executive officers. In the early 1970s, Jon Guthrie, whose missionary activity was invoked by Beal, Wilder, and Sessions as part of the argument for integration, became chaplain at Hendrix College, a position he would hold until June 1994 when he retired. Guthrie and others who would come to the college during the decade of the 1970s would bring new perspectives about the mission of the church to the world—one that was chastened about America's role in the world, and the degree to which Christian missionary activity had been captured by American imperialistic aspirations—and thereby model a humbler approach to proclaiming the gospel.

Of course, **the relationship between the North Arkansas Conference of the Methodist Church and the college *would also*** *change,*[32] but to provide a detailed account of how this occurred would take me beyond the scope of this paper. Perhaps the fact that Hendrix leaders began by looking to the conference for "leadership," and North Arkansas Conference leaders ultimately found themselves asking the college to exercise "responsible leadership" in the awareness that there was inadequate support for their views within the conference, indicates how the relationship between the church and the college had already changed.

Finally, it is worth noting that one of the reasons why the moral appeal of the three ministers was not persuasive was precisely because of what Rev. Aubry Walton had recognized five years before in the *first meeting* of the joint committee of Trustees and Hendrix faculty to explore the proposal to integrate Hendrix College. Namely, at the grass-roots level, the congregations of the North Arkansas Conference of The United Methodist Church would remain largely *segregated* communities of faith. In other words, the embodiment of the church's inclusive gospel to the principalities and powers (Ephesians 3:10) would remain largely absent in the places in Arkansas where the United Methodist interracial witness could have been most visibly present. By contrast, Hendrix College became one of the places where the procedures and practices of interracial hospitality slowly began to take root, but for a different set of reasons.

B. Responsible Leadership and the Providence of God: As one of my Jewish colleagues likes to remind me, whenever historians shine the spotlight on one set of circumstances, they fail to notice the ways that their narratives cast shadows that obscure the visibility of other events and personages. The danger of concluding that Marshall Steel "did the right thing for the wrong reasons" is that we make too much of his role in the process. As tempting as it is to decry the inadequacy of the actions that Marshall Steel and the board took, it would be a mistake to make that the primary focus of attention. As Steel himself might have recognized, the leadership that he exercised was simply the last in a sequence of conversations and decisions (on and off campus), the origins of which preceded his presidency. Similarly, if one reads A. W. Martin's call for "responsible leaders" who could practice "the principles and procedures" that would lead Arkansas Methodists out of "this wilderness of fear and prejudice" in a narrow way, it is all too likely that one will overlook the witness of those "saints" whose actions and interventions may have helped to shape the convictions of William M. Wilder and other future Arkansas Methodist leaders.

Conclusion

As I indicated at the beginning of this chapter, the story is richer and more complex than any of the historical accounts that have been written thus far. In the end, it is beyond our capacity to connect these elements of the larger story to one another, much less to provide an adequate account of the roles played by leaders of Hendrix College and/or the North Arkansas Conference of the Methodist Church in the integration struggle in the state of Arkansas.[33]

What we can do is pay attention to the effects of everyday practices and procedures in the present on the way we perceive our relationships with the past. For example, an indirect result of the demise of "separate but equal" in the public policy of the federal government has been the equivalent of a doctrine of "separate but equal"[34] *missions* for Hendrix College and the United Methodist Church in Arkansas. Segregated missions assume separate interests and project separate narrative plotlines, and therefore, such patterns can have a distorting effect on how we understand the seeds of change, as well as where we look for the origins of changes themselves.[35]

On the other hand, to refuse this kind of bifurcated thinking to structure how we read the role of Arkansas Methodists in the integration struggle means that we have to confront the fact that Hendrix College and The United Methodist Church in Arkansas continue to share some painful memories.

To recognize that the yearning expressed by leaders of Hendrix College and Arkansas Methodism in the 1950s to identify "responsible leadership" that could lead them out of the "wilderness of fear and prejudice" was also, at least in part, a product of the policies and procedures of racial integration is to confront distorted images of human leadership in relation to God's providential direction. For that matter, so is the disappointment that some Hendrix alumni and United Methodist leaders in Arkansas have felt about how and why Marshall Steel's actions occurred. If we are honest with ourselves, though, we have to acknowledge that the impulse to look for larger-than-life leaders whose actions are flawless is a form of wishful thinking. This kind of distorted thinking can also be paralyzing, particularly when the "heroes" for whom we yearn stand outside the everyday lives of those who look to them for leadership.

Instead of remaining mired in this kind of muddled thinking about ourselves and our shared history, we should remind ourselves that Christians are called to be *saints*, not heroes. As Anglican theologian Sam Wells has argued, hero stories tend to focus too much attention on individuals, as if their moral actions are self-constituted, and at the same time, such narratives can pay too little attention to the theological significance of "improvised" Christian witnesses.[36] By contrast, Well contends, stories about "saints" do not portray the individual actor at the center of the story because, after all, the story "is really about God" and what God is doing in human history.[37] To think of William Wilder's and Marshall Steel's actions in this context, I would argue, does not diminish their significance. Rather, it places their respective actions in the context of a wider saga that includes the stories of other moral actors.

Taking this theological perspective can also help us to see that while moral change may appear to occur as a function of individual performances, it is an illusion. To the extent that we prefer and perpetuate such distorted thinking, we impoverish our own moral imaginations about what it is possible to do and to be as Christian leaders. Such actions are better understood as improvised responses in a larger drama in which Christian "saints" are limited agents, part of a larger cast of characters, each one of which also stands on the stage of human history. Finally, it reminds us that the most notable feature of stories like these is the way God continues to use ordinary people *like us* to lead people like us out of the wilderness of fear and prejudice.[38]

End Notes

1. Others have recounted the experience of Linda Pondexter, the first African American to graduate from Hendrix in 1969. See James E. Lester, Jr., *Hendrix College: A Centennial History* (Hendrix College Centennial Committee: Hendrix College, Conway Arkansas, 1984).

2. See Hendrix College Archives, Paul Faris, "Minutes of the Meeting of the board of trustees," October 18, 1955, page 2. It is not clear whether the purpose of this committee shifted in the interim, or whether subsequent actions by the administration of the college reassigned this issue to a different committee. In any event, when the issues were taken up at the first meeting of the "Joint Committee," the framework of the discussion was not "enrollment" but "integration" and this is reflected in both sets of minutes on file in the Hendrix Archives.

3. There is reason to believe that this statement by the Hendrix faculty reflected deeply held religious and ethical convictions. For example, see the Hendrix College Archives for the related (undated—probably ca. 1956) "Memorandum to President Ellis Re: Integration" written by Prof. E. A. Spessard, which not only offers biological perspectives about why human beings segregate, but also reflects on ethical reasons, specific to Christianity, for why segregation should be banished from the Hendrix campus.

4. See Hendrix College Archives, Faris, "Minutes of the Joint Committee on Integration Representing the Hendrix College Faculty and Board of trustees," Jan. 3, 1956, page 1.

5. See summary of Paul Faris provided to President Marshall T. Steel (Feb. 1963), available from the Hendrix College Archives.

6. It is not clear what the sources of the internal quotations in this statement are. Attempts by the author to clarify this question have not yielded an answer.

7. Paul Faris, "Transcription of the Oral History Interview of William Curt Buthman," edited by R. W. Meriwether (1979), p. 81, available from the Hendrix College Archives.

8. William M. Wilder, letter to Marshall T. Steel, March 31, 1960, page 1. Available from the author.

9. A. W. Martin, letter to Charles McDonald, April 2, 1960, page 2. Available from the author.

10. Ibid.

11. There is no official list of persons who was present for this meeting. Participants recall that some or all of the following persons were present: Jim Beal, James T. Clemons, Ben Jordan, Charles McDonald, Johnny Miles, Sr., Robert Paul Sessions, and William M. Wilder.

12. As Jim Clemons recalls, when Steel was senior pastor of Highland Park Methodist Church, Dallas, Texas, he took several public stands in support of Civil Rights of minority citizens. First, during the early years of his ministry at Highland Park, Steel hired a social worker (who happened to be from Arkansas) to work with Hispanic immigrants and citizens in the barrios of Dallas, Texas. This was quite an unusual action at the time. In one other notable instance, Steel took a stand on the question of a controversial proposal for the citizens of Dallas to annex an area in which many poor Hispanic people lived. The consequences for the Hispanic people of the neighborhood in ques-

tion would be very significant. If annexation were to proceed, then water, sewage and other facilities would be constructed in that neighborhood; without annexation, they would likely continue to live in unsafe conditions. Marshall T. Steel preached a sermon on "The Good Samaritan" on the Sunday morning just before the referendum for annexation. Steel referred to the proposal and argued: "we cannot turn our backs on our neighbors." Clemons recalls hearing that the full sermon appeared in *The Dallas Morning News* the following Monday, the day before the election. Many leaders in Dallas credited Steel's sermon with having had a significant outcome in the election. I am grateful to Jim Clemons for calling these aspects of Marshall Steel's ministry to my attention.

13. This assessment was provided by one of the clergy members of the Little Rock Annual Conference, Dr. Aubrey Walton, who at that time was pastor of First Methodist Church in Little Rock. Walton, who had earlier served pastorates in the North Arkansas Conference (e.g. First Methodist Church in Searcy) subsequently was elected bishop (1960) and served the Louisiana area of the Methodist Church. See Faris, "Minutes of the Joint Committee on Integration Representing Hendrix College Faculty and Board of trustees," January 2, 1956, p. 1, available from the Hendrix College Archives.

14. Lester, *Hendrix College: A Centennial History*, 202.

15. In his letter of April 1, 1960, addressed to Charles McDonald, Fred Roebuck, another Methodist minister serving on the board of trustees at the time, described the role of Dr. Marshall T. Steel in the board's March 1960 deliberations. Our action in this matter was largely directed by some facts that Dr. Steel put before us. You recall that when the Methodist Student Group was in session in Russellville, they came out with a strong statement on the matter, and Hendrix College was involved. Dr. Steel said the mailman brought him many, many letters protesting integration and threatening to withdraw their children or not to let them enter next September if integration should be brought about. He said that it would greatly injure Hendrix College to attempt integration now as they need to build up a student body and the financial cooperation of people who are able to give to Hendrix in order to get going in a proper way

16. See Hendrix College Archives, "Minutes of the Meeting of the Hendrix College Board of trustees for March 13, 1962," p. 3.

17. See the full text of "Summary of President's Report to the Hendrix Board of trustees" (March 26, 1963), pages 2-4, available in Hendrix College Archives

18. Lester, *Hendrix College: A Centennial History*, p. 211.

19. As the Minutes of the meeting of the board of trustees of Hendrix College for March 18, 1964 made clear, Steel's pragmatic course involved no subterfuge.

"Dr. Steel pointed out that the admissions policy as provided in the Hendrix College By-Laws, is in the hands of the faculty. Therefore, the resolution which he was proposing to the board was a resolution authorizing the faculty committee on admissions to admit qualified students, rather than an instruction from the board of trustees concerning the admissions policy. He indicated that there should be a clear understanding that this was not subterfuge, and Dr. Steel indicated that if the board adopted the following resolution, the Admissions Committee of the College would admit qualified students regardless of race." (p 6).

20. Lester, *Hendrix College: A Centennial History*, 209.

21. The first record of the statement "Admission is not limited by race, creed, or national origin of the applicant" appearing in any Hendrix publications is found in the *1970-71 Hendrix College Catalogue*. I am grateful to Mrs. Delores Thompson, reference librarian at Hendrix College, for calling this fact to my attention.

22. Lester, *Hendrix College: A Centennial History*, 209.

23. The slippage between rhetoric and action was characteristic of Marshall Steel. When Marshall Steel addressed the Hendrix College community for the first time as President at the 1958 Convocation, he disavowed any intention of changing Hendrix. Yet already he had taken actions that would permanently alter the college's way of operating. See the related discussion in chapters eight and nine of Lester's *Hendrix College: A Centennial History*, pp.201-232 which in turn was based upon the faculty resolution of October 1955 in which the faculty sought the leadership of the church. Therefore, Steel would have had ready access to the very documents that demonstrated a different understanding of faculty prerogative. Second, there is no documentary evidence to demonstrate that Steel ever appealed to the board of trustees based on the arguments of the Methodist Church. All of the documented arguments he presented were based on secular appeals to fiscal responsibility, college procedure, and governmental regulations.

24. First, one month before the March 1963 meeting of the board of trustees, Steel asked Dean William C. Buthman to provide him with a summary of the 1956 faculty survey on integration.

25. Some observers would say it is a pattern that continues in the present in the way the leadership of the college deals with the leadership of the conference in an atmosphere not always marked by "mutual good will."

26. See Charles McDonald's correspondence with the Executive Director of the Methodist Children's Home of Arkansas, August 15, 1969 and Edwin Keith's response of August 29, 1969 and other related correspondence McDonald had with district superintendents and the bishop of the Arkansas in McDonald's personal file of correspondence. I am grateful to Charles McDonald for calling this aspect of the integration struggle to my attention.

27. The fact that younger people and/or "children" exercised leadership in the context of the Civil Rights movement has been the subject of several books. See David Halberstam, *The Children* (New York: Random House, 1998), a journalistic account of what happened to Diane Nash, John Lewis, and the other college students who initiated the Nashville sit-ins and who subsequently led the Freedom Rides through the American South in the early 1960s.

28. In this respect, The Methodist Church would not be alone. Before the decade of the 1960s was over, other sectors of mainline Protestantism would begin to register the seismic shifts that, in fact, had been altering congregational, conferential, and denominational structures since World War II. No book tells this story better and explains it sociological facets more thoroughly than Robert Wuthnow's study *The Restructuring of American Religion* (Princeton, NJ: Princeton University Press, 1988).

29. Although Angela Evans Benham is an example of the now well-documented pattern of "denominational switching" I do not mean to imply that she left the United Methodist Church because of changes brought about in the church as a result of the "integration" of the Central Jurisdiction (after 1968), or the election of African Americans to serve as bishops of predominately Euro-American conferences.

89

30. Wilder, Beal, et al. often used the word "establishment" for the leadership of the conference, particularly leaders like Sewell B. Wilford and Henry W. Goodloe who openly opposed integration.

31. While President Roy Schilling, Steel's successor had a seminary degree and at one time had been licensed as a Methodist minister, Schilling was not ordained and therefore was never a clergy member of either of the Arkansas conferences of the Methodist Church.

32. Over the next quarter of a century, Jim Beal, Charles McDonald and William M. Wilder, at different times, served on the board of trustees of Hendrix College, either as one of the trustees appointed for a quadrennium by the conference, or as a Trustee *ex officio* by virtue of the office held within the North Arkansas Conference.

33. The problem of how to narrate how leadership transpires in the midst of the messiness of human history is an ancient conundrum. It is visible in the book of Exodus, where the character of Moses is identified as a leader against the backdrop of various factors each of which seem to make it improbable that this Hebrew man would become the leader of his people. In 1 & 2 Samuel, the saga of how Saul and David were chosen to be kings of Israel is even more messy. One of the things that I love about the books of 1 & 2 Samuel is the fact that the editors of that two-volume work made no attempt to hide the contradictions. They laid them alongside one another. Contemporary American Protestants who are interested in gathering narratives of the involvement of church leaders in the Civil Rights movement could learn from the ancient Hebraic historians.

34. Here I have in mind the image of the shared hand and the separate fingers used by Booker T. Washington in his famous 1893 Atlanta Exposition Address. The application of this image to the relationship of Methodist Church to institutions of higher education may not be as strange as it initially seems, given the history of American Methodism and its still unresolved struggles with both segregation and its involvement with institutions of higher education.

I acknowledge that the inspiration for my use of this image in this context is Milton Sernett's study of *Black Religion and American Evangelicalism* (Metuchen, NJ: Scarecrow Press, 1972), where Sernett observes, "In matters of work and life, it is true, there were two different worlds in which white Christians and black Christians lived. But in matters of faith and order the Negro Churches reflected the structure and doctrines of Evangelical Protestantism. To borrow an image used by Booker T. Washington, black religion and white religion were as distinct as the five fingers of the hand, but they were one like the hand itself in sharing the Evangelical heritage."

35. I would argue, therefore, that the full story of what transpired in those years must include the collective journey of all the "saints"—black and white—of God who were associated with Hendrix College and the North Arkansas Conference (Southcentral Jurisdiction) and the Southwest Conference (Central Jurisdiction) of the Methodist Church.

36. Samuel Wells, *Improvisation: The Drama of Christian Ethics* (Grand Rapids, MI: Brazos Press, 2004), see chapters two and three, pp. 33-57. I cannot do justice to Wells' book in this context, but I would warmly commend his study to persons who are interested in reflecting about the meaning of human action in the context of Christian theological ethics. For a very helpful delineation of the differences between "saints" and "heroes," see pp. 42-44

37. Ibid., 43.

38. Many persons have assisted me with the research for this paper, more than is usually the case in research projects of this kind:

First, my late father-in-law, the Reverend Mr. William M. Wilder and The Reverend Dr. Charles McDonald allowed me to have access to their personal files for letters and documents concerning the integration struggle at Hendrix College. Bill Wilder, Charles McDonald, and Jim Beal each clarified technical matters related to their involvement in the struggle to integrate Hendrix College in several very helpful telephone conversations over the course of the spring and summer of 1994. In addition, Dr. James T. Clemons, retired Professor of New Testament at Wesley Theological Seminary, and former admissions recruiter at Hendrix College provided several helpful clarifications about the relationship of Hendrix College and the North Arkansas Conference based on his service in both organizations in the mid-to-late 1950s.

Library and archival assistance from several different archival sources has enabled me to complete this project in a timely way. First, Mrs. Dolores Thompson, of the Olin C. Bailey Library at Hendrix College went beyond the call of duty to provide research assistance and documents that I requested from the Hendrix Archives. And later, after reading an earlier draft of this essay, Dolores provided me with additional documents to support my argument. Second, Ms. Cynthia Burton, of the Pelletier Library at Allegheny College was extremely cooperative in arranging for me to have access to various materials from both of these libraries in Arkansas. As always, Cynthia was her cheerful self in the midst of dealing with my strange research requests.

Third, Jane Dennis and her staff at *The Arkansas United Methodist* newspaper were very helpful in locating an article about Angie Evans that was published in the predecessor news organ for the two conferences of Arkansas Methodism. I am also grateful to Mr. Robert Meriwether, Emeritus Professor of Education at Hendrix College, who pointed me to some of the oral history interviews available at Hendrix College, including several that he had done over the years with such figures as Marshall T. Steel. Bob Meriwether also assisted in other ways by giving wise counsel about the interpretation of events at Hendrix College based on his own vast experience as a historian of Hendrix College and Arkansas Methodism.

Finally, I am very grateful to those who took the time to read an earlier, very rough, draft of this paper. Jim Beal, Mary Wilder Cartwright, L. Gregory Jones, William M. Wilder, C. Jarrett Gray, Jr., each provided critical comments and corrections.

Into the Breech:
My Entry into Hendrix College
Linda Pondexter Chesterfield

In 1965, I graduated from Henry Clay Yerger High School in Hope, Arkansas. I had counted on graduating as either valedictorian or salutatorian of my class. That is all I had worked for during my high school years. Either of those rankings would have assured me of a scholarship to either Philander Smith College in Little Rock, Arkansas, or to Arkansas AM&N College in Pine Bluff, Arkansas. They were the only Historically Black Colleges of which I was aware in the state. And my world had been Afro-centered all of my life.

It was not to be. I graduated third in my class, and I don't know that anything was more devastating to me at the time. My grades were as good as the other two young ladies. We had been told that the hard courses—physics and chemistry—would count more than music, but it was all just a big lie. My mother went to the school to appeal the decision, but to no avail. I felt that I had let my family down, and I wasn't sure how I was going to go to college since my older brother, Ricky, was already there. We were nowhere close to affluent.

It never occurred to me that some papers I had filled out during the course of the year would lead to more than seventy-five scholarship offers from around the country. Heck, my teachers had to make me erase my pencil scribbling and rewrite my responses in ink. The National Merit Foundation instituted its National Achievement program to identify outstanding black students in the country. I became one of the first finalists. Amazing! That identification replaced my hopelessness with the promise of an opportunity for higher education. The National Achievement program stepped into the breech.

I wanted to attend Michigan State University. I am an avid football fan, and I was offered a scholarship at a football powerhouse. The transportation costs would have been huge for my family, so that thought went out the door. But, one of the schools that came calling was Hendrix College located in Conway, Arkansas. I had neither heard of

Hendrix, nor had I ever heard of Conway. But, I became acquainted with a wonderful man who came to Hope to recruit me. His name was Reverend Jim Major. He will always be special to me.

Later in my life when I served as president of the Arkansas Education Association, I had the great honor of presenting him the AEA Human and Civil Rights Award. He was also gracious enough to read scriptures in my wedding ceremony. His gentle persuasion helped me make the Hendrix decision. A higher education opportunity became a reality through him. Jim Major stepped into the breech.

Emily Johnson of Little Rock Horace Mann High School, a fellow finalist, was also recruited to Hendrix. She and I became the first African American students to attend the school, and we were roommates. Emily got married at the end of her freshman year and did not return to Hendrix.

I arrived in Conway via Trailways Bus Company. I remember wearing a green-figured empire waist dress that I had made myself, white tennis shoes and white socks. I was a true fashion statement. I felt as if I were sleep walking through that day. I had never been away from home, and I had never been in social settings with white folks. Jan Rhinehart, an upper classman at Hendrix, had made sure that I was invited to the Hope, Arkansas, picnic for freshmen. I'm not sure what I was thinking or feeling. I'm not sure if I was more scared or apprehensive. I was prepared to defend myself against whatever might come my way.

I felt I needed to be in defense mode both physically and mentally because I had taken my baby brother, Brack, to enroll in Paisley Elementary School in Hope, Arkansas. He and a young man named Jimmy Smith were desegregating their elementary school. I had just worked in the summer program with many of those same kids, and yet, they were jumping off the sidewalks as if my brother were dirty, and they were calling him names that just made me so angry. I almost dropped out of college before I got started.

When I arrived at the Conway bus station, I didn't have a clue as to where the college was, nor how I was supposed to get to it. But, there were three women at the bus station who seemed to know who I was. They were Dr. Ella Myrl Shanks, Dr. Helen Hughes, and Mrs. Lily Major, the wife of Rev. Major. I don't remember a thing about my journey from the bus station to Raney Hall. I don't remember walking to my room. I sure don't remember how that huge trunk I brought with me got up the stairs. I was just sleep walking. Those three ladies stepped into the breech.

My freshman year at Hendrix was marked by tears and laughter and adventure. I was on my own for the first time. I found my fellow Hendrixites kind, perplexing and some just down right nasty. I remember the kindness of Kay Denton when things got rough; I shed some tears and I wanted to go home. She helped to keep me there. I remember when my grandfather died, and I didn't know how I was going to get home. Joe Purvis told me to get in the car, and he and his girlfriend, Susan, took me home. I remember that Cookie Jones, Dan Dillard and Paul Guerin also made sure that I had a ride either to or from home. Jan Rhinehart, Buddy Villines, Randy Goodrum, Carroll Fowlkes, Catherine Fitch, to name a few, were just cool booties who made life easier. When I wanted to give up, one of these folks would step into the breech.

Then you had Catherine's boyfriend who would turn his face away from me and not say a word. You had people, some of whom were on Governor Clinton's staff or who represented black folks in court, who looked at me like I had something. There were those who would feed stray dogs on campus, but would not say a word to me. Curse me, hit me, but to deny my humanity was a cut most foul.

Meanwhile, I was doing an average job of getting acclimated to campus life. After all, I didn't have to be the brightest, I just had to pass. That's an attitude I regret now, because I could have learned so much more. Dean Shanks was my freshman college advisor. The ladies felt that it was important for Emily and me to have a woman with whom we could converse during our freshman year. I came to Hendrix as a history and political science major, so in my sophomore year my advisor became the one, the only, Robert W. Meriwether.

I was in awe of this giant of a man called Meriwether. He with the booming voice, the youthful look, and the great mind. The man always had time for me. It was he who had chaired a Constitutional Convention in which I got to participate. It was he who put the peanuts into the coke bottle and drank them together. It was he who taught us to argue both sides of an issue.

It was from Mr. Meriwether that I learned of the efforts of Dr. Marshall Steel, president of Hendrix, to make sure that the college was desegregated. I remember Mr. Meriwether telling me that Dr. Steel

wanted a unanimous vote from the board of trustees for the desegregation of the institution. He told me two board members abstained, but
Dr. Steel got his unanimous vote. Dr. Steel stepped into the breech.

Emily and I didn't just desegregate Hendrix College, we also desegregated Conway's First Methodist Church, the parent church of the
college. The pastor, Reverend Worth Gibson, and the board of trustees
of the church wanted to end its segregative ways. So Emily and I went
to church. Allidel Steel and I walked in together. You talk about feeling
as welcome as a snake in a chicken coop, boy! Allidel told me later that
she kept looking behind her to see if her slip was hanging, people were
looking at us so hard. I had developed the knack for seeing and not seeing by this time. It became another one of those sleep walking experiences. The faces were blurred, and I just remember a nice man preaching a sermon in a manner unlike that to which I was accustomed.

Emily's dad was a Methodist preacher, but I had to get up out of
there. It was so not like what church was supposed to be to me. I wanted to hear the piano and choir rock the house. I wanted to see and hear
the black preacher rev up the congregation. I went Black and Baptist.
When I got campused for thirty days, I went Black and Baptist almost
everyday to get off campus. "Hendrix ladies always wear hats."
"Hendrix ladies wear raincoats over their shorts when they leave the
dorm." "Hendrix ladies wear their beanies at all times." So much stuff
to disobey. So much stuff to get campused for. So much reason to wear
'em out when you act like you're going off campus anyway.

I do believe that our photos had been flashed to every entity in
Conway because everyone seemed to know who we were. Emily and I
were the only blacks allowed to enter the lobby of the movie theatre in
Conway. All of the other black folks had to go to the balcony to watch
the movies. We went to the movies via the lobby until we found out
that it was much cheaper to go to the balcony. This desegregation thing
only went as far as the dollars we had. We could go into any store and
try on clothing; that came later for other blacks. Hendrix was determined that whatever one Hendrix student could do, Emily and I could
do, too. Segregation loomed large and ugly in Conway, but to protect
us, Hendrix stepped into the breech.

I graduated from Hendrix in 1969, but it seems like only yesterday
that I arrived at a beautiful place for a difficult mission. My nieces,

LaRonda and Regina, are now Hendrix graduates. Some of my former students have graduated from there. I still go back to the campus to speak to students. I act as a mentor to black students on campus who also get discouraged. I feel it is my responsibility now to step into the breech.

Editors' Note:

   The Honorable Linda Pondexter Chesterfield resides in Little Rock and is a member of the Arkansas House of Representatives. In 2000, the Hendrix College Alumni Association named Mrs. Chesterfield an Outstanding Alumna.

All Are One in Christ

Frank Clemmons

I was appointed pastor of the Charleston Methodist Church in June 1965. Charleston, a middle- to upper-class suburb of Fort Smith, was a small town then, only about 2,500 people, and only about two percent of those were black. The public schools integrated with no problems prior to the Supreme Court's 1954 mandate. But the black community there, as well as the white, had dwindled, as there were few jobs in the area.

During the two years that followed my appointment there, I became acquainted with the few black families who lived just east of town. Three of the four families were active in the tiny African Methodist Episcopal Church (AME) located nearby. The fourth family had joined the Catholic Church.

The Charleston Methodist Church paid the apportionments for the AME congregation and assisted with the building's repairs. A black pastor from Little Rock conducted their services twice a month. However, I learned that the congregation was unhappy with the pastoral service they were receiving. To quote one of the members, "He comes on Sundays, preaches, takes our money, and goes back to Little Rock. He won't even come to our homes or eat Sunday dinner with us."

In the summer of 1967, after discussing it with others in the church, I invited the children from the AME congregation to participate in our Vacation Bible School at Charleston Methodist. They attended the whole week and felt welcome. Their parents attended the final event at the end of the week and felt comfortable enough to stay for refreshments.

Not long after that, I approached two families who were active in the AME congregation to ask if I could visit with the rest of their congregation about the possibility of their church joining with ours. We set up a meeting. Before the meeting was held, though, I visited with several key leaders in the Charleston Methodist Church. Among them was an eighty-year-old leader of the men's Bible class and bank president who said, "I'd love to have R.B. and Sterling in my Bible class." The local attorney, choir director, and chairman of the Committee on

Finance was also in agreement saying, "I sure could use Silvia and Etholia in our choir. Sure we may have a few who will object but it's the right thing to do." This local attorney was the future U.S. Senator from Arkansas, Dale Bumpers.

One after another of the church's leadership affirmed my decision to invite the black congregation to join ours. Only one of those I visited seriously objected, the beloved elderly teacher of the lady's Bible class. She very simply reaffirmed her conviction for the traditional separation of the races. "They'd be happier with their own place of worship," she said. Well, we talked most of one afternoon with me citing biblical and disciplinary affirmations of Christian equality and brotherhood. Finally, she said, "Well, Brother Frank, if you think it's the right thing to do, I won't object."

During my meeting a few days later with the whole AME congregation, there was some hesitation in accepting my invitation to join with the Charleston congregation. They were aware of the passing of the day when their small church was strong and vital in their community. Yet, they were conscious of the fact that their children were now being denied quality, Christian study and fellowship with children their own ages, they were not receiving caring pastoral leadership, and they had no one to play the piano and lead in music.

After a thorough discussion, one of the members said, "Brother Clemmons, won't some of the Charleston folks object to our being there?" I replied by sharing my visits with various church leaders affirming that the great majority would welcome them completely. But, I said, "Yes, there will be those who will object, and a few might quit attending because of their objections." She then said, "I couldn't live with myself if I thought I was the cause of one person leaving the church." I paused and said, "Victoria, you mean to tell me that you would deny your children good Christian education and fellowship because of the prejudices of a few narrow-minded people?"

"Brother Clemmons," she said, "when you put it like that I see no reason for our not joining up with you." Turning to the others, she asked, "What do you all think?" Having determined their approval, she said, "We'll be there on Sunday."

The response of the Charleston congregation was overwhelmingly affirmative as some fifteen black congregants began attending regularly with very little said. A white woman was miffed when some of the new attendees sat in "her pew," and a prominent farmer told me that "it's not right," but he kept attending. We only lost one white member due to the integration. Before the summer was over, I received eighteen black members into the church, and I might add that I did visit their homes for fellowship and pastoral care.

Two of my most meaningful moments in my pastoral career came as a result of the integration of the Charleston congregation. The first occurred in October on World Communion Sunday. As the congregation was coming to the altar, one of the black families was coming up the left center aisle just as the farmer who had so strongly objected to the integration, and his wife, were coming up the outside left aisle. When he saw that they would be forced to kneel beside the black family at the altar, he stopped stone cold refusing to move. His wife gave him a hard yank and they moved to the altar. He was kneeling right beside a black man. With tears flooding my eyes, I served *everyone* the body and blood of our Lord.

The second incident occurred when one of our older, black congregants was hospitalized in Fort Smith, a few miles away. I had visited him some in the hospital. Some of his extended family in Fort Smith invited their own black pastors to visit as well. The night the gentleman took a turn for the worst, he asked for his pastor. "Who do you mean, Poppa?" asked one of his children. "Why, Brother Clemmons, of course." I was called, and I went to his bedside where I prayed with him. We held hands as he died.

I conducted his funeral a few days later, which his children, grandchildren, and great-grandchildren all attended, plus nieces and nephews and a host of other relatives and friends. Some of them journeyed from St. Louis, Boston, Washington, D.C., Chicago, and Los Angeles—where there had been recent street riots, burning, looting, and much violence.

I couldn't help but think how a strange white man's message and ministry would be received. In my message I strongly affirmed that in an age when traditional values and morals were being abandoned, the life of R. B. Williams, Sr., represented the old fashioned virtues of honesty, integrity, hard work, and consideration for others. After the committal, each of the pall-bearers, all his grandsons, expressed their appreciation to me with not just a handshake but a full embrace.

I felt that one congregation and one pastor exemplified the words of the apostle Paul in Galatians, "There is neither Jew nor Greek, there is neither bond nor free, there is neither male nor female; for you are all one in Christ Jesus."

In closing, I must say that there were several reasons why the integration of the Charleston Methodist Church went so well. Both congregations had small memberships, and the black members were all known and well respected in the area. The public school integration went very smoothly. Also, I had been a pastor there for almost two years when this happened. I had gained the respect and confidence of the congregation and the community. I was not viewed as a radical sent there to force the issue. And finally, our actions were grounded in Scripture, in prayer, and in the authority of the *Book of Discipline*. Additionally, the district superintendent and the bishop knew nothing of our actions until after the fact, even though we were one of the first congregations in Arkansas, if not the first, to integrate.

But Then We Got a New Preacher
Jim Clemons

Segregation came easy in Wynne. On a piece of paper, draw a line left to right at midpoint of the page. Then draw a line top to bottom at midpoint. Three-quarters of the page represents whites. The northwest corner represents blacks. The lines of segregation in Wynne were clearly drawn and marked, thanks to the Missouri Pacific Railroad, with tracks east and west between Memphis and Little Rock and north and south between St. Louis and Helena, Arkansas, where a two-track ferry carried six rail cars and an engine back and forth across the Mississippi River each day. Growing up in this small, segregated, Arkansas town, I heard stories about lynchings and beatings, but I never saw one. I heard stories of Klan marches along the main streets, but I never saw one. What I did see were numerous acts of concern for individuals, over and over again.

My daddy was a sheet metal worker and roofer and often took me with him as he gave estimates, worked on new houses and repaired gutters and furnaces. In high school, I worked summers in his Wynne Tin Shop, putting hot tar roofs on schools and buildings. When rice became a major farm crop in the area, I cut the sheet metal, rolled, beaded and crimped the ends of hundreds of flume pipes that carried water from the wells to carefully sculptured dikes in the rice fields. Over the years, I worked side by side with several of Daddy's workers, including three black men, Leo Bass, James Beauregard and Sam Hardin.

At thirteen, I began delivering the *Arkansas Gazette*. My papers arrived on the train from Little Rock each morning at 5:00 a.m., if it was on time. My route took me to three city limits. A few black families subscribed to the paper, giving me my first, shocking entrance into Ward Four. As I biked along unpaved streets, with very few street lights, beside open, stinking sewage ditches that ran next to many homes, I thought of Leo, James, and Sam. This is where they lived. This is where they ate and slept, where they went to church, and to school, such as it was. This is what they came home to each day after work, along with domestics, janitors and railroad workers.

One cold Sunday afternoon, a fire alarm sounded. It was the newly built brick school for black children. A few of my friends and I ran several blocks to see it. Many other whites were already there. I said in the presence of some of them that I wish it could have been our old school, so we could get a new one. Immediately, one of the white adults looked me sternly in the face and said, "Son, don't you ever say that again!" I finally got the picture. Seeing a black school burn was nothing a white person should feel bad about. That was the way older people taught younger people, and the way I "had to be taught, carefully taught, to love and to hate" the right people. That is the way my education might have gone, on and on and on. But then we got a new preacher at the Methodist Church.

My first glimpse of Reverend Bob Bearden came just a few days after his move to Wynne from Walnut Ridge. Tall, thin as a rail, riding a bicycle with the seat raised as high as it would go. On his first Sunday in church, he entered the pulpit area in a frock-tailed coat, the likes of which I had never seen. When he sat down, he neatly folded the tails across his lap. I saw and felt the agony of defeat. What would my Baptist friends think of our having a preacher like that?

We sometimes compared our preachers, and the Baptists usually got the better of us. Brother Woodell was a handsome, friendly man, always showing up at school events, and a good preacher. Most important of all, he had been an all-conference end in football and often worked out with our team, coaching much of that time. But not to worry. Only a few months later, eight or ten of us were piled into a car riding around town, and we Methodists were talking about Brother Bearden's last sermon. One of our non-Methodist friends asked, "You mean you actually listen to what the preacher says?" We did.

With his wife Ellen he revitalized our youth group. She taught us square dancing, in the church basement, no less, and they were always welcoming when a few of us dropped by the parsonage unannounced to listen to their classical records. He took us to district youth meetings and to youth assemblies at Hendrix College about an hour away.

On a personal level, he taught me to play golf and took me with him on hot, sultry days to look for arrow heads, pots or bones along Crowley's Ridge to add to his Indian collection. In all his time with us, he was constantly seeking to expand our minds.

One night after our youth fellowship meeting, he asked me to stop by his office. He turned at once to his hope that I would enter the ministry, then asked me what I was interested in. I mentioned a few areas, but with no strong passion for any of them. He pointed out that ministers served in all of those areas—journalism, with reference to *The Arkansas Methodist*, chaplains in the navy, and college teachers. At some point, perhaps in a sermon, he mentioned that whenever a person decided to leave the ministry, the church viewed that decision just a sacred as the one to enter it. Not long after, he kept my parents after a Sunday evening service. When they returned to our car where I had been waiting, my dad said, "Jim, Brother Bearden wants you to go to Hendrix College."

Student days at Hendrix broadened my sensitivity to racial prejudice and my understanding of its evils. The atmosphere among faculty and students was open to liberal views, especially among the large number of pre-thes (before theology school) and others planning some form of Christian service careers. The guiding light for us was the beloved Dr. James Upton, Professor of Religion and Director of Religious Life. Two of my most memorable experiences came because of him.

Just before my first year ended, he asked me to represent Hendrix at a summer regional YM-YWCA meeting in Oklahoma. Arriving at the camp I went to my assigned cabin, where a few other students had already unpacked. Two of them were black, as were roughly one third of the hundred or so students attending. The whites mostly came from colleges and universities in the Southwest. The close relationship that developed over the week—sleeping, eating, studying, discussing, playing and worshipping together—reached my inner being in a far different way from the cerebral insights I had otherwise obtained. They were no doubt among the factors which later that summer led to my decision to enter the ministry.

The next year I went on a Methodist Youth Caravan. After ten days of training in Oskaloosa, Iowa, our team of four with Nola Smee, a youth worker from Kansas as counselor, began an arduous seven weeks in small congregations in her church's conference. There were no black students in the training sessions and none in the churches, but Nola's loving spirit and her stories about courageous blacks and the prejudice they endured in Florida where she had worked made deep impressions on me.

I finished my work at Hendrix in 1951 and that fall began seminary at Perkins School of Theology at Southern Methodist University. The next year brought the first integrated class to Perkins and the university. The change at Perkins came about because of the determined, bold leadership of its new Dean, Merrimon Cuninggim. His long, arduous struggle and the close cooperation of five black students are detailed in his brief account, *Perkins Led the Way* (1994).

I went to seminary expecting to focus on pastoral ministry, but in my first term I was in an Old Testament class taught by William A. Irwin, Professor Emeritus from The University of Chicago, where he was for many years a leader in historical criticism and one of the scholars that produced *The Revised Standard* version of the Old Testament. One term was all it took. Thereafter, I took every class I could get from him, including two summer sessions. With his encouragement, I later earned a doctorate in biblical studies at Duke University.

A second major influence on my life, totally unexpected, was the charismatic Joe Mathews at Perkins. Joe was convinced, and convinced many of his students, including me, that twentieth century theologians—Barth, Bonhoeffer, Bultman, the Niebuhrs, and Tillich—were "The Fathers" who were bringing about all the best that the Reformation was meant to be. My task now was to use Irwin's critical approach to scripture and Joe's passion for social justice, and to know in every sermon and crisis where I was coming from.

My first year back in Arkansas after seminary was as associate pastor with Bill Watson at First Church North Little Rock. The next year, I went to annual conference in Batesville, expecting to be reappointed to North Little Rock, but was told upon arrival that I was going to Widener-Round Pond, a four-point circuit on Crowley's Ridge near Forrest City. That's the way most pastor's learned they were moving in those days.

In the earliest days of my ministry, my thoughts returned to Bob Bearden and the way he went about doing ministry at our church in Wynne, while integrating the seminal biblical, theological and social foundations gained at Perkins. Three examples of his approach to promoting racial understanding and relations came to mind. Bob and Brother Woodell organized the first ministerial alliance in Wynne. From the beginning, they extended invitations to two black pastors to join them for study, devotions and preacher talk on a regular basis, meeting in each others' homes so they could also eat together.

On another occasion, Brother Bearden announced in church that a quartet of black men would be singing at the evening service. There was not a large crowd, and the singing was not that of the Wings Over Jordan Choir. But once the quartet had sung, they returned to their seats on the front row for the rest of the service. It was the first time blacks had attended regular worship at our church.

Later that year, he told a group of us youth that he would be preaching one Sunday afternoon at the black Methodist church and invited us to come with him and to sing in the service. It so happened that there were five of us: a pianist, soprano, alto, tenor and baritone. We sang and were very cordially received, even though no one compared us to the Wings Over Jordan either. It was the first time any of us had worshipped in a black church. Again, he was expanding our minds.

In the spring of 1956, two years after *Brown v. Board of Education*, my youth group at Widener Methodist Church was scheduled to host a sub-district meeting. Our youth and I agreed the program would focus on the coming of integration. We had two young people from Forrest City High and a high school history teacher from Wynne to speak. The youth spoke of the need for understanding, and the teacher on the history of the Supreme Court arguments and decision. After the presentations, there were questions and discussion.

The meeting was going very well, alleviating my initial anxieties. Then, one of my prominent adult leaders got up and walked out of the sanctuary, slamming the door behind him. That was bad enough, but what really scared me was when he came back in and took a seat up front.

Soon after the discussions began, he rose and spoke very forthrightly about his feelings that integration was wrong and the very thought of it angered him. He sat down without further comment and stayed through the end of the meeting. Fortunately, he and I continued to have a good relationship the rest of the year, and he said, when my appointment to that church ended, that he respected me as a pastor and as a man. But I had no reason to think he had changed his mind about integration.

Before leaving Widener, I had a call from Hendrix President Matt L. Ellis, inviting me to join the college admissions staff. I accepted.

Besides seeking to increase enrollment, my duties soon included directing the alumni office, improving school-church relations, some fundraising and occasional teaching. I made no effort to recruit black students, though I did join a group of mostly younger ministers who met with Dr. Marshall Steel, who came in February 1958, to urge Hendrix to integrate. The later history of Hendrix is addressed in other articles presented here by Michael Cartwright, Linda Pondexter Chesterfield, and Jim Major.

In 1960, I left employment at Hendrix to attend Duke University, earning my doctorate in Biblical Studies. In 1963, I became Chaplain to the College, Assistant Professor and Director of Student Life at Morningside, a United Methodist school in Sioux City, Iowa. I organized a group of students to march in Selma, Alabama.

From 1967-1995, I was on the faculty of Wesley Theological Seminary in Washington, D.C. Integration was always a topic in classes and student meetings. While participating in a major march on Washington in the spring of 1968, I encountered, for the first time, caustic attacks on whites who considered themselves there to support The Movement. Within a few weeks I had published in a leading Methodist magazine, "What Next for the White Liberal?"

My ministry has been significantly shaped by outstanding teachers, stimulating colleagues and inquisitive, insightful students, who have brought joys and rewards I could never have imagined, none of which would have been possible had we not gotten that new preacher, Bob Bearden.

Making History Through Taking Pictures
Jim Clemons

Since the beginning of photography in the nineteenth century, humans blessed with sight have marveled at the new worlds "picture takers" have opened for them. Views from outer space and from within the tiniest portions of our brains are seen everyday, informing our minds, reforming our thoughts, transforming our hearts and lives. We take them for granted.

So, too, pictures of our lives together: a peace treaty being signed on the deck of the USS Missouri; a burning child running naked through a village street in Viet Nam; one small step for the man on the moon; the successful landing of a "troubled" space shuttle; a plane crashing into the World Trade Center. Some of these moments, among all the moments of all the peoples of the world, we call "historic."

September 4, 1957, was one of them. What the desegregation of Little Rock Central High School was, has become, and what it will continue to be, is linked directly to the courage, the artistry, the genius, of one of those "picture takers," Will Counts.

On that day he was a young photographer for the *Arkansas Democrat* in Little Rock, now the *Arkansas Democrat-Gazette*. He sensed that what was about to happen at Little Rock CHS would be newsworthy and was on hand when Elizabeth Eckford, the first of the black students to arrive, tried to pass through a row of Arkansas National Guardsmen who stood with bayonets fixed to their rifles.

He was also at the spot where Alex Wilson, one of three Negro newsmen, a former U. S. Marine and later a war correspondent in Korea, was chased, beaten and viciously kicked. (His picture, and others, are in the pages that follow.) When President Dwight Eisenhower saw the picture, after having tried to negotiate between Orval Faubus and Congressman Brooks Hays to resolve the issue, he reportedly said, "I've got to do something." In the 1960s, Counts' picture of Alex Wilson was selected by the National Press Photographers Association

107

and the University of Missouri as one of the fifty outstanding news photographs of the century.

The day after seeing that picture, Eisenhower ordered the Arkansas state guard to be nationalized, putting them directly under his orders as commander-in-chief, and 1,200 troops of the 101st Airborne Division arrived at Little Rock Central High. Most of the time they were on duty with fixed bayonets.

What happened at Little Rock Central High School that day was a historic moment. It changed history, and Will Counts, "picture taker," in a unique way helped make it so.

Editors' Note:

Will Counts later became a distinguished professor of photographic journalism at Indiana University. In 1999, its university press published his A Life is More Than a Moment. As of 2002, six of Counts' former students had won a total of seven Pulitzer Prizes, and others had earned top honors at the national Hearst Awards and various other competitions.

Will Counts took the following pictures in September 1957, reprinted with the permission of Vivian Counts and the Indiana University Press. For more pictures and more on this story, see his book, *A Life is More than a Moment* (Indiana University Press, 1999).

As Elizabeth Eckford approached Little Rock Central High School in September 1957 to become the first black student to enroll, she was turned away by the Arkansas National Guardsmen. A white student was allowed to pass through their line as Elizabeth approached.

After Elizabeth was denied entrance into CHS, she made her way to a city bus stop where she was comforted by New York Times *education reporter Benjamin Fine. He sat with her for a moment and advised her not to let them see her cry. Fine is pictured here wearing the bowtie.*

Hazel Bryan, wearing the white dress behind Elizabeth, walked among the integration protesters as they heckled the black students. Hazel had come that morning with her parents. Only a few of the protesters were CHS students. Hazel and Elizabeth met again on the fortieth anniversary celebration of the integration event. Hazel had the opportunity to apologize to Elizabeth face-to-face for the hateful things she said that day in 1957.

Elizabeth and Hazel in front of Little Rock Central High School on the for-tieth anniversary of the integration.

112

Mr. Alex Wilson, a former U.S. Marine, Korean War correspondent, and a top Civil Rights reporter, was at CHS September 23, 1957, as the Little Rock Nine were finally able to enter the school. Near 16th and Park Streets, he was surrounded by a white, segregationist mob and brutally kicked and beaten. He was able to get back to his car safely, though. He said later, "Yes, I was abused—a victim of misguided violence—but I am not bitter. If my effort to help bring human dignity in its fullest sense to the oppressed minority here is successful, then the welfare of all will be enhanced."

Reconciliation
Vivian Counts

What was it like when Will and I made the "reconciliation" picture of Elizabeth Eckford and Hazel Bryant at Little Rock Central High School forty years after its integration? You know the original black and white version: the one in which Hazel is walking behind Elizabeth with a terrible sneer on her face as Elizabeth makes her way to the high school. Will and I got them together in 1997, years after the traumatic event.

It was a beautiful, warm, autumn day. Will and I had come to Little Rock for the fortieth anniversary of Central High School's integration. Will and I had driven our friends' van to meet with the women because it had an Arkansas license plate and our car had an Indiana University plate. Will was concerned someone from the newspaper would spot us. We didn't want this meeting to be public or a photo opportunity. We parked at the high school museum and waited for Hazel to arrive so we could go to Elizabeth's house together.

I was eager to see Hazel and wondered if we would recognize her. When she pulled into the parking lot next to us, I remember thinking how very attractive she was. I hugged her and told her how wonderful I thought it was that she was willing to face Elizabeth and apologize to her face to face. Hazel told us that she called Elizabeth many years ago and apologized to her over the phone. Elizabeth remembered the call, but didn't know which white girl Hazel was since there were several girls screaming horrible things while following behind her that day.

We drove to Elizabeth's house in the borrowed van. I remember taking Hazel's hand and walking with her up to the door. Elizabeth opened the door to us. Hazel was the first to speak. She said, "Thank you for letting me come today." Elizabeth responded, "You are very brave to want to face the media again." With that said, we walked into the cool house, comfortably decorated. The wall-to-wall bookcases gave it that warm, lived-in feeling. I thought to myself that this woman is right after my heart; she loves books.

Elizabeth hadn't chosen what to wear for the photo and asked if we would help her decide. It seemed so natural to be talking about clothes. We helped her pick out the navy blue dress with the red vest from several she showed us. While we were looking at clothes, we started talking about her beautiful irises blooming beside her door. Before we knew it, we were totally engrossed in sharing with each other the kinds of irises we had in our own gardens. Elizabeth made it so easy to chat. She didn't want the attention to be on her and would guide the conversation so it included everyone.

My dear husband was sitting there amazed at how easy the three of us talked about flowers, children, and grandchildren, just as if we were old classmates getting together again. The three of us were about the same age and had been school girls in the fifties, but at very different schools. Will had to hurry us along. I think we chatted for a very long time.

Will had discussed with us where he wanted the shot to be made. He wanted the two women chatting in front of the high school where the traumatic even happened forty years ago. My role as the photographer's wife was to talk to the subjects being photographed and help them feel relaxed so they would not pay attention to the camera. I didn't have to work too hard at that. The two of them started talking, and Elizabeth told Hazel something funny and they started giggling. Will got that shot.

I don't remember a lot of what happened after the photographs were taken. I do remember that we went back to the van and talked for a long time. Hazel told us she had been so embarrassed about her photograph being taken with that ugly sneer on her face. She said, "You know, life is more than a moment." I remember Will and I talking about how profound that statement was, and it eventually became the title of his book about the integration.

Will was more proud of that photograph of these two women than any other photograph he ever made. Not that it was so perfectly composed or that the light was just right, but because of what it represented. The beautiful gift of forgiveness, of an attempt to reconcile the terrible things Hazel screamed at Elizabeth on that fateful day in September 1957.

Will had several opportunities later to share this moment with different groups. It was, however, in the fellowship hall of our church, The First United Methodist Church of Bloomington, Indiana, where the idea for a book was born. One of our good friends, Zig Zigler, a member of Will's Covenant Disciple group and an editor at The Indiana University Press, was present at the program and urged Will to write a book telling the whole story of the integration crisis in Little Rock. And as they say, "the rest is history."

The Lingering Aftermath
Joel Cooper

I became pastor of Little Rock's downtown Winfield Methodist Church in 1961 after ten successful years at First Methodist Church in Conway. Winfield had become Arkansas's largest Methodist church in the years following World War II. This was the result of two things. First, the church had enjoyed some wonderfully effective ministers during that time, and, second, the community around the church was one of the few areas in which returning veterans and their families, mostly white, could find housing. They joined Winfield by the hundreds.

But as new communities developed in the suburbs of Little Rock, those families began to move out of the downtown area and join churches nearer their new homes. As the white families were moving into the suburbs, black families were moving into the vacant housing in the downtown area. By the time I was assigned to Winfield, it had been losing members for some time, although it was still a very strong church. In my five years there, I did not help the situation much, if any.

Winfield was well situated in an old, established neighborhood, but the anticipated movement of African Americans into the church's vicinity, combined with the typical southern attitude toward integration, had put fear into the hearts of many of the remaining members that the church would integrate or become entirely black. Even before my arrival at Winfield, I received letters which told me in no uncertain terms that Winfield intended to remain a white church. Of course the letter writers did not represent all of the church members, but they did represent a significant minority.

I have included three of those letters here to help you understand the quality of the air people were breathing in Little Rock and the state, even four years after the Little Rock Central High School debacle. The following letter came from an anonymous author in May of 1961:

> Welcome to Winfield and we wish you at least four happy years here, and we think that is entirely possible. However, Winfield like most other churches is upset and is being torn apart by extreme left

wing groups that have invaded our churches. In our opinion the national Council of Churches is dominated by out and out communists (if not they sure are first cousins). Also, Aldersgate and Philander Smith are merely workshops for the teaching of communism (sit-ins, kneel-ins, freedom rides, mob violence, etc.). All under the guise of religion.

We are not surprised that a Negro was elected president of the Ministerial Association. However, our current pastor assured us at the time (about six years ago) the association integrated that it was a gesture of friendship only. If the preachers really believed that then they are a lot dumber than their members. You can help build our church back up by denouncing the NCC and by ignoring the Negro issue.

We are sick and disgusted with all the stupid mess. We are all white members and we intend to remain all white and that includes our pastor.

Another letter came in 1964:

You know it is hard for me to conceive of a minister of the Gospel creating as much dissent and disharmony in a church as you have created in Winfield. I was led to believe that the Methodist Church was the most democratic church of any denomination. I was also led to believe that a Methodist minister would listen to the recommendations of the majority of his board members. It seems that I have been grossly mistaken in both of these beliefs. I grant you your right to your belief, but I question your right to try to force your belief on 1,500 members of Winfield Church....

The integration issue came to a head in Winfield when a group of Philander Smith College students decided to visit various white churches on Sunday mornings in Little Rock to find out if they would be seated for worship services. Ultimately, it was part of a movement to bring African Americans into the main stream of American life and to treat them like the citizens the *Constitution* declared them to be. On more than one Sunday, I watched from my study as ushers meet Philander Smith students at the steps of our church, but would not seat them for worship.

This was one of the lowest periods of my ministry. I had no choice by to keep on keeping on, but I was treading fast to keep my head above water. I did not want to split the church. I wanted to work through the problem with the congregation. What could I do? The answer came in a statement I made to a called session of the Administrative Board at Winfield in the fall of 1963 (paraphrased):

Soon after being assigned to Winfield, I had a meeting with the church's Policy Committee. From what was said at that time, I understood that the church had no formal policy regarding Negro visitors. However, last spring two Negro students from Philander Smith College were turned away from a Sunday morning worship service. At a second meeting with the Policy Committee, I was told that Winfield did have a policy against seating Negroes that dated back many years. It was then that I openly expressed my conviction that such a policy is morally wrong. The committee discussed the matter with church members in a series of meetings, in which I stated my opinions again. The committee decided that nothing was being accomplished in the meetings and no more were held.

The issue presented itself again this fall when two students from Philander Smith again were denied entrance to one of our worship services. I was not notified the students were coming on either occasion. It is clear the direction in which this church has taken. Already in this city, a number of Methodist Churches are seating Negroes with very little stir. That is the direction in which the Methodist Church is going. I ask you to follow your Church.

As pastors, we believe that we best serve the Church when we preach and work for the things we feel to be God's will. And in this case, with the *Book of Discipline*, the Council of Bishops, and the Methodist Church-at-large behind us, we have every reason to proceed. I ask you to follow your Church.

I want you to know that I have not attempted to organize board members to support me in what I am saying tonight so that I could impose my position upon you. I have no way to enforce what I am suggesting and have sought no way. I am asking, as your pastor, that each man in his own mind and heart, closeted away from the pressures of what his peers may think, decide what should be done under God. Your decisions will be registered by our actions in the days to come. I appeal to you to stay steady and use your influence to steady others. Take the attitude of "wait and see. My church and I may not agree, but I will wait and see." There need be no loss of members in this church. Other churches currently seating Negro members have not experienced great loss of membership. Each of you is as good a church member as they. You have demonstrated this in other areas. I believe we can get over this hurdle and onto other important issues.

After soul-searching and prayer, and by the authority given to me as pastor by the *Book of Discipline*, I respectfully request each of you, in his own church position, to follow the law and spirit of The Methodist Church by seating and accepting all visitors to our services without regard to color.

It would be an understatement to say that I did not convince everyone with my presentation. Within a day or so I received a letter informing me that I should "slow up" on the issue of blacks attending our church, and that several members will leave the church if the ushers choose to seat them when there are "three other good Negro churches in our part of town, and as you know, it is the church members who pay your salary." Both myself and the bishop regularly received letters such as this. He answered their letters and strongly supported me. There was even an organized effort to force my hand by members withholding their pledges.

After four years at Winfield, the Bishop asked me to stay one more year so that those objecting to my stand would not feel as if they forced me to move. I stayed another year. Some Winfield members did indeed move their memberships, but the majority remained there. However, the issue of seating Negroes was not resolved during my time there.

Integration was the dominant issue at Winfield the entire five years I served that wonderful church. I took my stand where the Church stands. If there had not been a strong support system for me and my wife, Bill, including wonderful lay people, my district superintendent and my bishop, I would have died there, professionally and physically. I am greatly indebted to them.

Summer Camp
Ronald W. Durham

I grew up in Jonesboro, Arkansas, where I attended Jonesboro High School. At that time, it was an all-white school, which left me unprepared for special opportunities that awaited me. After high school, I enrolled in Arkansas State College, now Arkansas State University, and won a summer scholarship to Inspiration Point Fine Arts Colony in Eureka Springs, Arkansas. I was a bit anxious, as I had only been away from home to attend scout camp.

Upon arrival at the Colony late one Saturday evening, I found my bunkmates were all men older than I was. In the bunk next to mine, there was a black man from Oklahoma City. As he walked through the bunkhouse at night, all you could see was his Saint Christopher medal shining in the moonlight.

The next day, in order to get acquainted, we met to share our talents with the group. I sang my aria and felt very proud of myself. A black man followed me. He sang the best tenor aria I had ever heard. Then he sat down at the piano and played a piece from Stravinsky, followed by a wonderful piece on the cello. I felt that he had more talent in his little finger than I had in my whole body. I wasn't sure what to think or what to do. This was all new to me then.

That night, many of us rode the bus into town to see a movie together. The usher collecting the tickets informed my black friend that he had to sit in the balcony with the other blacks. We objected, but my new friend insisted we not create a scene. So, we went to our seats downstairs, and he went to his seat in the balcony.

The next weekend, a black girl who played in the orchestra with me, asked me if she could go to the movies with us because she didn't want to go and sit by herself. Without thinking, I said, "You won't have to sit by yourself." When we got to the theatre, we were told the same thing as the week before. This time, however, again without thinking, I replied, "We are all going in together or we're not going in at all. We bring twenty to twenty-five people here every Saturday night, and if we leave, we will not be back." Somehow, after a short wait, we were all seated together, downstairs. It had never been done in Eureka Springs. We hadn't planned it. We just did what we thought was right.

On weekends, most of us, black and white, would go into town to do our laundry. We would put our clothes in the washers and then go into the downtown area to shop. We started with a large group, but as we walked along, some would go into this store and some would go into another. On this occasion, I went into an old-time barber shop for a haircut. As I waited for my turn, a man came running into the shop, slamming the door behind him. Out of breath, he related how he had just seen a six-foot-two-inch black guy come out of the hotel up the street with a blond lady, and he kissed her hand right there on the street for everyone to see. Turns out, he had not kissed her hand but was only smelling a new perfume she had just purchased! As I got into the barber chair, one of my black friends from the Colony walked in. She walked over to my chair and offered me a donut. You could have heard a pin drop ten miles away.

I learned a lot about myself that summer, as well as a lot about a world that I had known little or nothing about. I learned to see people for what they were or could be, not for what they looked like or their skin color. As a result, my perspective changed far easier than for those in much of our country in those days, and for some even now.

Sitting-In in Medical School
M. Joycelyn Elders, M.D.

During the height of the Civil Rights movement (1956-1966), my contribution to the movement was not "sitting-in" at lunch counters, riding on restricted seats on buses or marching in protests; rather, I participated in a different way, while always remaining supportive and grateful to those who were making the way possible for me to be where I was.

I "sat-in" in medical school trying to prepare myself to take a seat at the table of human rights. The lack of education, healthcare, family planning, immunizations, and opportunity, as well as poor drinking water, correctable disabilities, and severe poverty prevented so many black people from being able to take their rightful places in society. These conditions framed the society in which I grew up.

I came from a family of poor sharecroppers, the oldest of eight children, and had never seen a doctor prior to entering Philander Smith College in Little Rock. When my brother had a ruptured appendix, my father put him on the back of a mule to take him to the doctor. However, the doctor said that he couldn't hospitalize a black person, so he just drained the pus out of his abdomen and sent him home. I watched as my aunt died of spinal meningitis without the benefit of treatment by a doctor. Her back became increasingly arched and she bent back almost double before she finally died. My best friend and her sisters had crossed-eyes and suffered a lifetime of teasing and ridicule because of their disability that easily could have been repaired by a doctor. It is heartbreaking to look back on those times when the people I knew did not have access to healthcare only because they were poor and black. I always wanted to do everything I could to change this.

The catalyst that propelled me from the cotton patch to college came in the form of a white, Methodist woman who spoke at my church, Tabernacle C.M.E., about how black people could go to college at Philander Smith, a Methodist institution. She said that there were scholarships for women through what is now the United Methodist Women. I felt hope stir inside me in a way that was new. Shortly after my sixteenth birthday, my supportive family picked cotton to earn the money for my bus fare to Little Rock so that I could register at Philander Smith College. Since I had attended a one-room school in my early years and passed grades at my own pace, I was able to graduate from high school early at age fifteen.

I will always remember the look in the eyes of my younger brother, Chester, exhausted after working in that cotton field all day with all of us, who looked up at me and asked, "Do we have enough yet?" I promised myself right then to help every one of my brothers and sisters who wanted to go to college. Wearing a new dress my aunt had made, I packed my cardboard suitcase and left for Philander Smith College. It was all because a Methodist woman cared enough to travel to the small town of Schaal, Arkansas, to talk to some poor black people about college opportunities. Who knows what a few encouraging words can do to an eager heart?

After hearing Dr. Edith Irby Jones speak when I was a freshman at Philander, I knew that I wanted to be a doctor. Many people have asked me if I always wanted to be a doctor. I remind them that you can't be what you can't see; we did not even see doctors on television, because not only did we not have a TV, there was no television reception in my area of Arkansas until after I was in college. When I graduated from college and did not have any money, I joined the U.S. Army looking forward to using the GI Bill for medical school. In the Army, I was trained as a physical therapist, then spent the remainder of my three years of service (1953-1956) in the Women's Medical Specialist Corps.

Since it was before the time of student loans, only people with money to pay for tuition, books and living expenses could attend medical school. But I found a way by using the GI Bill, working summers, plus help from my Uncle Reva, and a part-time job on Saturdays at the McRae Tuberculosis Sanatorium in Alexander beginning in my sophomore year. The TB Sanatorium was run by an internationally renowned authority on TB, Dr. Hugh Browne, an excellent physician, teacher and mentor.

There were three black students in my freshman class in medical school at the University of Arkansas in the fall of 1956, and there was one in the sophomore and junior classes and three in the senior class. It seemed almost a miracle to me that I could be there at all. In the course of my orientation to medical school, I and the two other black medical school freshmen were told that we were to eat with the other Negro people at the medical center. It turned out they were all maintenance, housekeeping and cafeteria workers. There were no black professionals there. We did not think that segregating us for meals was extraordinary, since this was the order of things at that time, especially in the South. In southwest Arkansas, we did not eat out. There were no restaurants for us except the back door, and we didn't have the money anyway.

The University of Arkansas Medical School had a dance and banquet for seniors in 1960 that was held at the Little Rock Country Club. Just before the event, the black students were informed that we would not be allowed to attend, and we were offered $30.00 each in reparation. It was many years before the social order had changed enough to make it safe or comfortable to eat in any restaurant we might choose.

Segregation was the way society was organized and there was not much time spent discussing it in depth. Certainly, the black community keenly felt the unfairness of the separate and unequal treatment, but little had been accomplished to successfully challenge the long-established system of injustice. I cannot imagine that anyone living under such conditions, either white or black, could truthfully say that segregation was separate but equal in practice. The black part of the separation was inferior or more inconvenient, if it existed at all.

The order of things began to change, however, with the 1957 Central High School crisis, which became a successful challenge to segregation—primarily because it televised racism for all to see. According to my white friends who experienced the 1957 Central High School crisis from another angle, whites were uncomfortable with their images portrayed this way on TV, while blacks were amazed to see the conflict broadcast into living rooms across the world. Even those who knew little about the geography of the United States had now heard of Little Rock and seen the images. The view was not flattering. People listened, and most of all watched, as Chet Huntley and David Brinkley induced bystanders to comment on public school integration by the Little Rock Nine as they walked through the crowds of often-heckling, hostile, white students and parents.

As the state government moved to squelch the successful defiance brought by children trying to go to school, the federal government moved to block the state. Central High School was closed, and the reality of hundreds of white students without a school, the injustice of racism, and taxation without benefit were only small matters compared to the successful defiance of segregation by the black community to the Arkansas legislature and perhaps to most white Arkansans. When Central High was reopened with the presence of the National Guard, which President Dwight Eisenhower called up to ensure that the Little Rock Nine were able to enter the school, the gaze of the world continued to be focused on the racism in the South and in Arkansas. It became embarrassing and even humiliating to some white people who viewed the protesters, their fellow Arkansans, as buffoons.

The University of Arkansas Medical School was not untouched by the turmoil. Having lost face and power, the Arkansas legislature responded by deciding that state funds should be paid to train only white doctors. When all faculty members were required to sign a loyalty oath stating that they were not communists or be fired in order for the Medical School to retain their funding through the state of Arkansas, numerous people began an exodus. The conventional southern view in this McCarthy-era was that being supportive of integration was the equivalent of being communist. Of course, all of the faculty members were well-educated persons, and quite a few were not from the South. So, they were appalled by the injustice in which they were required to participate knowingly. They had been participating in segregation both by living and working in a segregated area, but likely without being as conscious of the situation prior to 1957.

At one point, the Arkansas legislature proposed the idea of utilizing local medical doctors as teachers to successfully carry out the three missions of the medical school: education, research and patient care. Of course, they recognized neither the caliber of professors who were there, nor the complexities of the subject matter and the training required to teach graduate studies in medicine. For about fifteen years, the legislature threatened to eliminate funding from the University of Arkansas Medical School at Little Rock. As an alternative, it proposed funding an all-white medical school in Conway at the already established Arkansas State Teachers' College, now the University of Central Arkansas. The proposals, needless to say, never happened.

Integration of the two "E's" (education and eating) seemed to be at the forefront of political unrest during the desegregation of Central

High School. For black medical students, the barrier of not being able to eat in the cafeteria with our classmates was addressed by the dean of the medical school. He issued a statement that all of the medical students were equal and would be allowed to eat together.

I immediately took advantage of this new right. As I entered the cafeteria for the first time, and bought my lunch, I spotted a table where some of my classmates were sitting. As I approached to eat with them, one said, "I'm not going to eat with no "nigger." He loaded up his tray and angrily huffed off. From that day forward, I continued to eat with the classmates I knew the best, but always avoided any table where he was sitting.

Most people fall in the middle of the racist spectrum, but a few despicable and remarkable people are to be found at each extreme. Even before we were allowed to eat with the white students, there were some folk around who appeared to understand the discomfort and injustice that segregated eating brings. A pediatric nurse, Jo Herring, suggested that we both bring our lunches, and we ate together in an office.

During my senior year, a faculty member thought she was paying me a compliment when she told me, "Why, you have as much education as some white people." I countered by saying that actually I had more education than most white people.

My freshman year, I shared a duplex with a white classmate, Lilly Ann Farley. She was confronted by neighbors declaring that she couldn't live with me because I was black. She told them that was fine and that she would move if they would pay her rent. We never heard from them again. Both of us were so poor that year that we did not even have a telephone.

For my internship, I went to Minnesota, but returned to the University of Arkansas Medical Center for my pediatric residency. When I was a second-year resident, the Southern Society of Pediatric Research meeting was held in Memphis. Dr. Alice Beard, a pediatrician at the University of Arkansas Medical Center, and I traveled there and shared a room at the Peabody Hotel. We usually ate there, but one morning, we went to a little restaurant close to the hotel. We were sitting there waiting to be served, when someone came up and said to me, "We are sorry but we can't serve you." Dr. Beard replied, "But she's a doctor, just like me." He elaborated, "We just don't serve nigras." She was more angry and disturbed by the treatment than I was, since I knew there was always the possibility of something like that happening.

Often, white people did not know about the treatment that blacks received in eating establishments and other places until they were actually confronted with it face-to-face.

Even in 1964 and 1965, staff from the pediatric research floor planned parties that were held only in the labs because they had such difficulty finding restaurants that would serve black people. When I was chosen Chief Resident of Pediatrics at the University of Arkansas Medical Center, I suspect that much preparation had to be done prior to any announcement. Dr. Ted Panos, the chair of pediatrics probably spoke to the other department chairs and the nine pediatric house officers. They were the finest group that he had ever assembled and selecting a black, female chief resident seemed to me to be quite a risk. I can imagine that he spoke to Dr. Sam Boellner, a fine physician who interned at Vanderbilt and influenced three other young physicians to come to Arkansas with him. He was and is a person of integrity, a leader. Although I do not know what was said, since they were behind me and supported me the entire year without exception, I think he must have said something like, "Dr. Elders is our chief and we will support and respect her and make certain that everyone else respects her." I was there seven days a week, probably twelve hours a day, and it was a wonderful time in my life. It was such a remarkable thing to be chosen as chief resident that *Jet* and *Ebony* magazines and a national CBS news program highlighted the news with profiles on my family and me. Now, when any of those nine former residents see me, they still call me "Chief."

After my residency, when I became a research fellow with Dr. Edwin Hughes, Dean Horace Marvin invited my husband, Oliver, and me to his home for dinner to meet a visiting dignitary. I think this may have been the first time I had eaten at a white person's home. The dignitary asked me what I had done to help "my people." I replied that I had gone to medical school for them.

I hope that my "sit-in" time in medical school had some positive effect on black women and men, and poor people in general, who want to become doctors and join other professions that seem out-of-reach. That United Methodist woman planted a seed that she never knew would grow into the life that I have had the privilege of living.

Editors' Note:

M. Joycelyn Elders was appointed Surgeon General of the United States of America by President William Jefferson Clinton. She was the first African American and the first woman to serve in that office.

Venturing Out
Dick Haltom

I began my years of ministry as an associate minister of the First Methodist Church in Pasadena, Texas, in 1962 when Paul Martin was bishop of the Texas conference. My ministry in Arkansas began in 1963 when I was ordained as an elder in the North Arkansas conference. My first assignments were to organize two new churches, Hendricks Hills Church in Fort Smith and then one in Indian Hills, a rapidly developing section of North Little Rock. The church at Indian Hills eventually merged with First United Methodist Church to become First United Methodist Church of North Little Rock. It was here that I became active in the Civil Rights and anti-war movements.

During my stay at First Methodist Church in North Little Rock, I was chairperson of the peace division of the Conference Board of Church and Society. In the summer of 1964, we organized a group of about five people from Arkansas that would eventually go door-to-door in Holly Springs, Mississippi, registering blacks to vote. Our training for such an assignment was at First Methodist Church in Memphis. We were trained by noted Civil Rights leaders such as Reverend James Lawson, a black Methodist pastor serving in Memphis, and Reverend Will Campbell, a Baptist radical who was called The Prophet.

While in Memphis, several of us went to a movie starring Sidney Poitier at a theatre on Beale Street. I believe the film was *Lilies of the Field*. It was a frightening experience for us as whites, for the theatre was filled with African Americans. It was also frightening in that time, and unusual, to travel in a vehicle with blacks. These are things we pay no attention to now, but at the time, it was very different.

The Aftermath: One Mother's Story
Pat Wood House

I was in my mid-twenties and living in Little Rock at the time of the crisis at Little Rock Central High School. I had children in the public high schools and a son in second grade. One evening an older couple whom we knew well came to our home to talk about the troubles with desegregation. They wanted to go to court to stop plans for integrating the elementary schools, and asked if our son could be the plaintiff. My husband and I were appalled that they would dare ask, and as firmly and politely as we could said we would not even think of using our son in this way.

They failed in their effort to promote segregation. What they accomplished instead was to make me decide I had to do something to stop the destruction of our schools. When Governor Faubus closed the high schools, I met with a group in the home of Adolphine Terry, the widow of former Congressman David D. Terry, to form the Women's Emergency Committee to Open Our Schools.

My involvement in that work needs to be seen in the larger context of the times. I was frequently struck by the sharp contrasts within the religious communities. We attended one of the largest churches in Little Rock, where the pastor was highly regarded as a preacher and very popular with the congregation. He asked if I would be on the Committee for Social Action, which I was honored to do, in spite of my age and inexperience among the older, more well- established members.

I was keenly disappointed during the first meeting to hear only a short discussion of a prepared motion on how to cover the electrical wires for Sunday morning television broadcasts so that the elderly would not trip over them. No mention of our response to the crisis at our doorstep, and indeed, in my living room. The church had already decided not to get involved, as if the cry was, "Rome is burning! Hail, Caesar!" when it should have been, "Rome is burning! To your posts! Save every man, woman and child!" Thereafter, the sermons seemed to be little more than beautiful, safe platitudes.

By contrast, the Reverend Richard B. Hardie, pastor of Westover Hills Presbyterian Church, was speaking out clearly and forcefully for integration. There was dissension among his members, some of whom left his church. But he stayed, and later, the street that led to the church was named for him out of respect and appreciation for his ministry.

Another person actively speaking out through letters to the editor of the *Arkansas Gazette* was "Hardscrabble." No name was associated with this pseudonym for years, but it gradually became known that the writer was Dr. Richard Yates, professor of history at Hendrix College. The letters were later published by the college with full attestation to one of its beloved faculty members.

Unlike the split among church leaders, the Women's Committee was united in purpose. From the beginning we agreed that our sole focus would be on opening the schools, something all parties could agree on. We came up with the motto, "Not integration, not segregation, but education." We began at once to recruit new members, to meet with both black and white Parent-Teacher Associations throughout the cities, and with black pastors, attorneys, physicians and other respected leaders in the black community. We grew, but it wasn't just a piece of cake. Several of our hardest workers asked that we not mail anything to their homes for fear of repercussions.

We decided we needed to reach a larger population and asked radio and television stations to run spot announcements we had prepared. All but two gave us an immediate and firm "No!" One of the longtime KLRA morning radio hosts was Hal Weber, who took the role of "Brother Hal," a countrified feller who told lots of jokes and was popular with a group we couldn't reach otherwise. When we approached Mr. Weber, he immediately said, "Yes, I'll be happy to do your spots," which he did sometimes more than once a day.

Eventually, one of the television stations was sold and the new owners agreed not only to use our public service announcements but also to give blocks of time for panel discussions. Once we decided to have a panel on education. I called Dr. Yates, who had been one of my favorite professors at Hendrix, to be on that program. When he said he could not accept the invitation, I broke down and cried over the phone. He was moved by that response and said, "All right. I'll do it." He spoke on the beginnings of education in America. There were no public schools and only the rich could get an education. The panel went on to ask, "Do we want to go back to education only for the rich, or do we decide now that our schools will be for everyone?"

The turning point in our effort was our research on the financial impact the school crisis was having on the city. We published our results showing that not only were families leaving, but that far fewer people were coming in; facts the business leaders simply could not ignore. What became known as "The Little Rock Report" was widely read in other states, and we received calls from New Orleans, Louisiana, and Atlanta, Georgia, asking for our assistance as they began their efforts to keep their schools open.

After the school closures, the local segregationist school board fired forty of the cities finest principals and teachers. The widely used reason was only that they were all "nigger lovers." This action brought many more women to our cause, especially mothers who knew and admired the educators personally. Soon thereafter, it was time for an election to choose new school board members for those whose terms had expired. We found three people to run and had to elect all three to get the majority necessary to rehire those who had been fired. We organized a campaign and worked very hard to get black voters to turn out. At the time, Arkansas had a poll tax to be paid by each voter, a real barrier for so many poor blacks. We worked very hard, organizing groups to knock on every door and to provide transportation to the polls. On election night we gathered in a large downtown hotel to await the results. Our candidates won by a margin of less than one percent

National publicity came from many major newspapers, including *The New York Times*. On September 10, 1962, *Life* magazine came out with a special issue on "The Takeover Generation." It pictured one hundred people. Four of the people pictured had full-page photographs. I was one of the four.

My political activism brought problems to my family. My husband was a representative of one of the country's leading pharmaceutical companies. When I received the national publicity for seeking integration, his corporate headquarters in another state called their district representative in Memphis and told him to stop me because it was hurting business. He called my husband and invited us to dinner at a nice restaurant, during which he said in a very friendly way that I was hurting sales and that if I did not stop, it could cost my husband his job. He left knowing that I had no intention of stopping and that my husband would not try to stop me. Once the home office realized that they were threatening a national leader in sales and that his productivity had not dropped during the time I was active, they decided not to say anything further to us.

Later I helped get a grant to establish a new radio station that would be aired primarily to reach people with moderate and low incomes, most of whom were black. In August 1984, station KABF 88.3 FM began, giving a voice to that group of listeners every day and every night. Our format was much like that of National Public Radio stations today, with open lines for call-ins and discussions on relevant topics. I served as Chairman of the station for twenty-one years.

Along the way, I drafted the Arkansas voter registration act, as required by President Lyndon B. Johnson's national legislation requiring all states to eliminate the poll tax or any form of required payment for the privilege of voting.

Fiftieth Anniversary of the Desegregation of Little Rock Central High School

Chester Jones

We mark the occasion of September 25, for on that date in 1957 regular army troops from the 101ˢᵗ Airborne Division in Fort Campbell, Kentucky, were sent into Little Rock to permit nine black children into Central High School. This move came after President Eisenhower had been unsuccessful in persuading the Arkansas governor, Orval Faubus, to give up his efforts to block the court-ordered desegregation plan for the school. Governor Faubus had given in to the southern tradition of state-sponsored Jim Crow by refusing to halt interference with the federal court order to desegregate the school. This forced the president to send in federal troops to put down the mob action and integrate Central High. The confrontation has been called one of the most serious state/federal clashes in modern times.

The students who integrated Central High School later became known as the Little Rock Nine. Daisy Bates, the president of the NAACP at that time, mentored and advised them about how to succeed in their mission to enroll in the high school and not compromise their principles.

These were difficult times for people of color in Arkansas, and also for me, as I recall those times growing up on a small farm in rural, southwest Arkansas. The path to public school integration in Arkansas was painful, and the hills were hard to climb as I remember catching the yellow bus each morning in our town of Mineral Springs. We passed by the high school closest to me, which was white, and rode the bus ten miles to the black high school in Tollette, Arkansas.

During my last three years in high school, 1957-1960, I was fortunate to have two exceptional and socially conscious homeroom teachers. They kept the class informed about what was happening in the world. We were also made aware of current events by the five-minute newsreel, shown at the Elberta drive-in movie theater before the main feature.

135

Also, I had uncles who had served in the Army during the Korean War; they came back to share with my family a global view of the world. There were also many white people of goodwill who stood up against racial segregation and made serious sacrifices for the cause of truth.

But my understanding of the world was as a 14-year-old boy growing up in rural Arkansas, never thinking about challenging the southern ritual and tradition of the so-called "separate but equal" society; that is, until two things happened that changed the course of my life.

First, I had a homeroom teacher who had graduated from Philander Smith College, a small, black United Methodist-related college in Little Rock. Mr. Burns kept us informed about current events and how the world and the South were both going through some changing times. He discussed with us the brutal lynching of 14-year-old Emmett Till in Money, Mississippi. Emmett had been killed in a brutal slaying for allegedly making an advance toward a young, white woman. This incident, more than any other, served as a capstone to the revision of my earlier understanding of the assertion made in *The Declaration of Independence*, that "all men are created equal." Now I was forced to reinterpret that assertion to say, "all except blacks."

Nevertheless, my homeroom teacher would have our class, almost every day, repeat together the reverent words from the *Declaration*— "We hold these Truths to be self-evident, that all Men are created equal, that they are endowed by their Creator with certain unalienable Rights, that among these are Life, Liberty, and the Pursuit of Happiness …" I am still grateful for Mr. Burns, who never allowed us as a class, during the struggle for racial justice and social equality, to be blinded by bigotry and prejudice. He knew such a reaction would produce warped thinking and racial hatred that would allow anyone to interpret the *Declaration* in ways other than "all (men) people are created equal."

I now know that racial hate is not a one-way street. Racism infects both the hater and the hated. I am glad that my parents, my church and my homeroom teacher did not allow me to be blinded by the racism, prejudice and bigotry that can create a climate where the hated learns to hate the hater.

My homeroom teacher believed in the promised fulfillment of our destiny as one nation "under God." He believed this even at a time when the long shadow of racial oppression and resistance hovered over

Central High School in Little Rock. He believed that President Eisenhower, and not Governor Faubus, would one day, with the help of God, define who we were as a nation. He believed that all people are created equal as sons and daughters of God. He read Rudyard Kipling to us, who said, "If you can keep your head when all about you are losing theirs and blaming it on you, if you can trust yourself when all men doubt you ...," which taught us that the struggle for equality and racial justice was not in vain.

And because of their faith, people like my parents, folks from my church, and my homeroom teacher lived to see our nation come to a great juncture, where the last sanctuary of American jurisprudence, the U.S. Supreme Court, said in the May 17, 1954, case of *Brown v. Board of Education* (Topeka, Kansas) that racial segregation in public schools was unconstitutional. That historic decision overruled the 1896 *Plessy v. Ferguson* case and declared that separate educational facilities were inherently unequal. A great deal of the credit behind the *Brown* decision, and many other decisions for racial justice and equal educational opportunities in America, is due to the legal work of the NAACP lawyers, headed by Thurgood Marshall.

Another turning point in my life during the 1957 crisis in Little Rock came with my sister, Joycelyn Elders. She was attending medical school that fall, and always seemed to find a way in her mind to live beyond the segregated reality found in the South at that time. The best example of her beliefs and early struggle against Jim Crow racism and segregation happened at the Elberta drive-in movie in Nashville, Arkansas.

Joycelyn had taken us to the movies to see *Old Yeller*. Made by Walt Disney in the 1950s, the film was about a poor Texas family in the 1860s and a wonderful dog, Old Yeller. It was a movie that paralleled so much of what life was like for us growing up as sharecroppers in southwest Arkansas. However, the warmth and love of this memorable movie has also left in my memory the racial incident that almost caused us to miss the film. It all began after my sister had purchased the tickets for herself, my two younger sisters, and me.

We were told to park, as usual, in the back section reserved for the "Coloreds." Joycelyn, however, refused at first to park there and instead parked near the last row reserved for whites. After she parked, an attendant came and asked her what she thought she was doing? "You know you can't park here; that's the rule," he said. I was afraid and puzzled. I could see that Joycelyn was hurt and angry, the angriest I had ever seen her. She didn't understand why, when she had paid for her tickets the same as everyone else, she should be forced to park in the back. I wondered what on earth they had done to her mind in Little Rock at Philander Smith College. I feared for our safety, and even our lives, when Joycelyn told the attendant that she would leave before she would move all the way back in the "Colored Section." By this time, my little sisters and I had begun to cry, partly out of fear, and perhaps largely because we didn't want to miss the movie due to what I then thought of as my sister's insane stubbornness. We cried and begged and finally Joycelyn gave in and moved the car back a couple of rows, and she grudgingly stayed to see the movie.

When I think back on this incident, I am pained by the cruel realities of racial prejudice that were part of our growing up. At the same time, I am proud to have a sister like Joycelyn, who has never believed that discrimination was right or acceptable on any level, for any reason. She has always stood up for what she knew to be right. It is her uncompromising stance for what is right and true that has carried her far, and which has also caused problems for her along the way. But she has been willing to pay the price required in order to maintain a stand for what is right.

While I would have been happy to watch the movie through a peephole at the back of the theater, Joycelyn refused to compromise her belief that it was wrong to have a double standard for black and white then, and it is wrong now. But I and millions of other children since 1957 were the eventual beneficiaries of the courage and commitment to justice and equality demonstrated by Joycelyn and the Little Rock Nine.

One question always remains, and that, of course, is: Where do we go from here? As we mark the 50th anniversary of the forced integration of Central High School, we must ask how our past and present stories can come together to shape the future of quality education in Arkansas. As we plan ahead, we must address the question that has often held us back: How can we say that we hold essential principles of equality that we know to be right, and at the same time permit practices of inequality and institutional racism that we know to be wrong?

In light of this occasion, I have tried to reflect briefly on some of my recollections. I am once again reminded that we must work together to build a better present, to show that we are serious about moving public education forward in Arkansas, which presently ranks 37th among the states in public education. To do this, all persons in Arkansas need to have a sense of hope and feelings of ownership, responsibility, and power to help make our public schools all they can be. What is our vision for promoting inclusive quality education in Arkansas? I am encouraged by the positive attitudes and hopeful signs that I see expressed at many levels, where people are working together. Our future must be based on a hope and reality that is greater than us. Let us put our hope and faith in the Lord, who will lead us all into a new future.

Editors' Note:

Chester Jones is currently an Associate General Secretary of The United Methodist General Board of Church and Society, serving as Executive Secretary of the Commission on Religion and Race.

Jesus Loves Me
Carlotta LaNier

I've often made the statement that I have been a Methodist all my life. My faith in God was tested in 1957 as I and eight students integrated Little Rock Central High School. I can unequivocally say that my upbringing in the Methodist Church, the lessons learned in Sunday school, the singing of "Jesus Loves Me, This I Know," along with the support of my parents, family, community and history, made it possible for me to rise above all the ugliness of that time.

We had the opportunity to attend Central High School because of the Supreme Court decision *Brown v. Board of Education*. Times were changing, and Virgil Blossom, superintendent of Little Rock public schools, had a plan to slowly integrate its schools. I did not understand then the details of just how slowly he meant for integration to happen. In reflection, the plan was to build two new high schools and then integrate LRCHS. My chance to declare Central as my high school choice came in the spring of my final year at Dunbar Middle School. It seemed the logical thing to do. It was so logical, so expected, that I do not recall even talking about it when I got home. However, that simple declaration, as it turned out, has made all the difference in my life since.

I entered Central High School in the fall of 1957 with eight other students. The group included three sophomores: Gloria Ray, Jefferson Thomas and myself; five juniors: Melba Patillo, Thelma Mothershed, Elizabeth Eckford, Terrence Roberts, and Minnijean Brown; and one senior, Ernest Green. At the time, I knew some of them well, others I knew casually, and a few, I didn't know at all. We were not nine students who knew each other. We were nine students who shared a skin color, an address that made Central our neighborhood school, and a desire to obtain an education that was the best in Little Rock at the time. Over the years, we all have developed a close and rich relationship.

For thirty years, most of us made seldom and rare trips back to Little Rock. The NAACP held their national board meeting in Little Rock in 1987, and they decided to invite all of us back as their guests. We were brought together that morning at the library inside the school. The president of the student body, Derrick Noble, and an African American male student greeted us. Little Rock mayor, Lottie Shackleford, an African American woman, was there to welcome us as well. She had been in Ernie's class in 1957, but chose to stay at Horace Mann High School because she was editor of the yearbook. Central students escorted us through the halls of the high school. I had been back to the school only once since leaving on May 30, 1960, after graduation. It was not easy for us to walk those halls again because it was impossible to stop the flood of sad memories from our teenage years.

When Bill Clinton, who had been a sixth grade student in Hope when we climbed the steps to become the first African American students to enter Central High School, was governor of Arkansas, we were all invited back to Little Rock as his guests. One night during our stay in Little Rock, Governor Clinton invited us to the governor's mansion, and Hillary Clinton got out of her sick bed to welcome us. This warm and welcoming hospitality was a striking contrast to my last interaction with an Arkansas governor, Orval Faubus.

Melba Patillo Beals recalls our thirtieth anniversary gathering in the opening of her 1994 book *Warriors Don't Cry*. Her book was the first to tell the story of that year from the point of view of one of the Little Rock Nine. But there were nine students, and, therefore, of course, nine stories. Our first day at Central on September 4, 1957, was easy for me. I think I felt secure being surrounded by the Little Rock Ministerial Alliance and other leaders in the community. I didn't like what I heard when we reached 14th and Park streets, but I still felt confident because the Arkansas National Guard was to protect the citizens of Little Rock (myself being one) and those of the cloth who were with me. History has documented all that took place that day and the subsequent three weeks, with President Eisenhower finally calling out the best, the 101st Airborne, the elite paratroopers, to escort and protect us as we entered Central High School.

My senior year happened without military escort. Thirteen African American students were then enrolled at Central with Jefferson and me, the two remaining of the Little Rock Nine. But that year did see residual events stemming from the 1957-1958 school year. My home was bombed in February 1960 with my family in bed. I was quoted as saying

I would not let this stop me from going to school. I would continue or die trying. I believed in God's protection and that God had created us equally. I surmised that some people had not gotten the message.

I became the only female of the Little Rock Nine to actually participate in graduation exercises. I completed my senior year after spending the 1958-1959 year getting my education the best way I could, mostly through University of Arkansas correspondence courses. I went on to graduate from Colorado State College and did not talk about my experience at Central for the next thirty years. Today I serve on the board of trustees of my alma mater, delivering the spring 2006 commencement speech, and on the board of trustees of Iliff School of Theology, a United Methodist Institution.

These commitments reflect a thankfulness for support from my ministers at Whites Memorial Methodist Church, Wesley Chapel, Bethel A.M.E, and Union A.M.E., to name a few. Churches played a big role in those days and were quite involved in our foundation for doing the right thing. Leadership was found in the church through Dr. Cox, Dr. Martin Luther King, Jr., Rev. Harry Bass, Rev. Young, Rev. Dryver, and Rev. Henderson, to name only a few. They reminded me "Jesus does love me." This is written in their honor.

Incident at Dermott
Mary Ann Lee

In the summer of 1965, I accepted a position directing youth at the Methodist Church in Dermott, a small community in southeast Arkansas. I had just completed my first year of study at Perkins School of Theology at Southern Methodist University in Dallas. Little did I realize the life-changing impact that summer job would have on my life, the church at Dermott, and the community-at-large.

During my first year in seminary, I had participated in Civil Rights marches as well as in many discussions about race relations. As a Christian, I felt that if I was to be true to the Christian faith, I had a responsibility to stand up for equal and compassionate treatment of all people, regardless of race, color, ethnic background, or creed. In my seminary classes, we enjoyed a healthy exchange of controversial ideas, including those concerning race relations and civil rights. That was not to be the atmosphere at Dermott.

The editorial page of the *Arkansas Gazette* on June 23, 1965, began, "Miss Mary Ann Lee has been banished after the briefest but most 'controversial' of tenures as youth director of the Methodist Church of Dermott, thus ending a racial crisis of undetermined—and by now indeterminable—proportions." Of all places where I thought one should be able to discuss God's word, as well as its message for social issues of the day, the church stood out to me as a beacon of light. Surely one could speak there and search for the truth in an atmosphere of honesty and acceptance, whether there was agreement or not. To this day, I have struggled to understand how my words could have triggered such a controversy in the first place, a controversy that would lead to my immediate dismissal.

On a Saturday morning in June 1965 I led a Bible study class for a group of teenagers at Dermott Methodist Church and proclaimed that God loved everyone, regardless of race, color, or creed. This was a statement that had been recited so frequently that it had become a cliché, even in the 1960s, for many members of our society. To a community where racial prejudice loomed large and where school integration was to take place that fall, such a statement was heretical. I asked the young people what that statement meant to them. Instead of hearing the anticipated response that we were all different with different gifts, I was hit head-on with *the issue*!

An immediate and sarcastic response from a seventeen-year-old boy quickly informed me that God does not love everyone: "God don't love them niggers cause they ain't nothin' but animals." There were snickers and laughter. I tried to defuse the hostile environment created by that comment by pointing out that we all, regardless of race, color, or creed, might act like animals at times but that, nevertheless, every single person had the potential to become a child of God, to accept the gift which had come through and in Jesus Christ.

Needless to say, the statements of a youth director who had been there only ten days could not penetrate the years of accumulated prejudice and hatred. I was quickly labeled a "nigger lover" and was immediately equated with "all them sex maniacs and perverts who went on freedom marches." In spite of the fact that I tried to explain to them that I had marched in Dallas with completely different motives than those of which they accused me, my comments aroused only curiosity and hatred.

Feeling that the issue had gone far enough when several youngsters made statements such as, "We ought to round them all up and send them back to Africa," and "We ain't goin' to school with no snotty-nose niggers," etc., I closed the session with a prayer. I included a statement that it was not my purpose to force my ideas on them, but rather to encourage them to come to grips with the real meaning of the Christian faith for their own lives, to examine their own hearts and motives through study of the Bible.

The first indication of an attitude which was to lead to my dismissal by Sunday night came when I tried to purchase a cup of coffee at the local drugstore on Saturday evening at eight o'clock. The news that I was a "nigger lover who had marched in one of those freedom marches" spread to every crack and crevice of that town with the rapidity of a kerosene fire. It was only after a lengthy conversation among the employees that I was served the cup of coffee. They didn't have to say anything. I felt their dislike for me, even though we didn't know each other personally. I spent that night in prayer, not knowing what I would have to face the next day.

All evening I kept wondering if there was something else I could have said to those young people that would have made a real difference.

On Sunday morning, I was met with icy stares as I stood behind the pulpit to read the Scripture and deliver the morning prayer. The atmosphere from that moment on was saturated with hatred and rejection. I was called a "nigger lover" to my face on church property. The preacher was receiving non-stop phone calls about my racial views and was apparently told to fire me immediately. One hour before the Methodist Youth Fellowship was to meet that night, the teenage girl who was to present the program called saying that she could not come to the church because her mother objected to my presence there. The mother said, "As long as that youth director is a nigger lover and is in this church, my kid isn't going to set a foot in it." Instead of the thirty-five people who were to be present at MYF, only ten actually came.

When the *Arkansas Gazette* called the minister, he told the reporter that "the 'crisis' was only the tiniest of teapot tempests, but that it was racial." Additionally, the paper reported him as saying, "She said she didn't want to hurt the program of the church ... and since the racial matter is tense here, we, the Board, the officials, thought it might be better if she terminated her position." All I had been told was that it would be "safer" if I left. The concern for my safety was such an issue, even though this was denied by the Dermott paper, I was moved out of my office at the church and the rooming house by midnight and kept safely at the parsonage until 3:45 a.m. when I left town without having been given a single opportunity to meet with a board member or any other adult at that church. I made an effort to talk to the board, but I was told that they knew my views and didn't need to talk to me.

To be called a "nigger lover" to my face on the church's property, to be equated with "sex maniacs and perverts," and to be told by the minister that it would be "safer" if I left in the middle of the night, are experiences which filled me with both pity and regret. Most of all, it was heartbreaking to see the young people being intellectually and spiritually suffocated, being encouraged, in fact, victimized, to carry on a deeply entrenched tradition of hatred and prejudice. The only thing more disheartening for me was to see the local church give an indication of tacit agreement to that tradition when its purpose and basic beliefs were so much at odds with that kind of attitude.

Once word of my dismissal hit the local newspapers, there began a lengthy period of controversy with an editorial in the June 23, 1965, issue of the *Arkansas Gazette*, letters to the editor, comments by the people of Dermott, and statements by church leaders and by colleagues from Perkins. The paper continued to run articles about the "The Incident at Dermott" throughout the summer.

The voice of Methodism rang loud and clear when Bishop Paul Galloway made a public statement to the press on my behalf. Certainly these statements on my behalf were gratifying to the extent that they revealed evidence of increased understanding and growth with respect to the race issue in Arkansas, especially in the leadership of the Methodist Church. There were, however, other statements that disturbed me because they gave indication of being so one-sided. Hatred for the Negro was replaced with hatred for those who hated the Negro. It was so difficult to get across to people during that time, and perhaps even today, that hate multiplied by hate does not and cannot, under any circumstance, equal love.

Criticism is a vital factor in Christian growth. This is a truth which few Christians would fail to support, and it was certainly needed in the Dermott situation. But criticism combined with bitterness can be nothing short of catastrophic in the final analysis. There also has to be a time for listening and healing. As I wrote in *The Perkins Log* in October 1965, "The word of love will continue to be distorted and rejected in other Dermotts, for changes cannot be made overnight, but somewhere along the way there is evidence that the word was not spoken without a listener." Evidence of that, in my case, came from a newspaper clipping and an anonymous letter from someone in Dermott. It read, "Dermott schools opened this week on an integrated basis without incident." The letter simply said, "Thank you for standing up for love in this town."

Integrating Hendrix College
Jim Major

I was born in Conway in 1916 and finished high school at Central High in Little Rock. I attended Little Rock Junior College, now the University of Arkansas at Little Rock, earning my school money by working as a youth minister at Winfield Methodist Church. I finished college at Hendrix and earned a Master of Divinity degree at Duke University.

In 1960, after several years as pastor of Methodist churches in Arkansas and as a missionary pastor of a Spanish-speaking church in Santiago, Chili, with my wife, Lillie Rainey Major of Little Rock, I was asked by Dr. Marshall T. Steel to come to Hendrix College as Vice President and Director of Development. In that capacity, I established the first Alumni Loyalty campaign and the Parents of Graduates campaign.

At the time, Hendrix was struggling with the issue of integration, largely because of a group of Methodist pastors, most of them young, who were pushing for Hendrix to accept black students. They brought resolutions to the North Arkansas Annual Conference, in which Hendrix was located, and met with both President Steel and with the Hendrix College Board of Trustees. The pastor whose name I recall as one of the leaders was Jim Beal. At one point, it seemed that the group was threatening stronger conference action if the school did not integrate.

Although Hendrix never had an official statement barring black students from attending, the custom had always been not to invite them. Dr. Steel decided it was time to recruit black students from Arkansas high schools. I was not in the recruiting office, but he wanted me to recruit black students, which was necessary if Hendrix was to get a large grant from the Ford Foundation. He said to offer any black student a full scholarship, provided they could do the work academically. At the time, Hendrix required all applicants to take the College Board exams. The scores on this national test were one of several factors in the Admissions Committee's deliberations, though certainly not the only one.

I was concerned about where the scholarship money would come from, but he just said, in his typical fashion, "Do it!" He left the job up to me. I began by getting a list of North Central accredited high schools and spent a year visiting those in Conway, Little Rock, Pine Bluff, Fort Smith, Arkadelphia, Magnolia and Hope. The school principals were usually open, wanting their students to have this opportunity, but some, understandably, kept me at arm's length. My presentations included telling them that Hendrix was an excellent liberal arts college and that full scholarships would be provided to those accepted. I would then ask if they had any questions.

I was very disappointed that after all my visits, we had only two students, both women, to apply for the fall term of 1965, Linda Pondexter from Hope and Emily Johnson, the daughter of a Methodist minister, from Little Rock. But before Linda would agree to attend in the fall, I had to speak with her grandmother for approval. I went to her home, where she, her grandmother and I sat in a bedroom, the only place large enough for us to talk together. Her grandmother said that she thought it would be good if Linda went of Hendrix, and so she did. Linda was the first black student to complete a degree at Hendrix. She is a remarkable person and an excellent public speaker. In her last year as president of the Arkansas Education Association, I received a special award from them for my efforts in bettering race relations. Linda is now an Arkansas state representative from Little Rock.

Several other black students have come to Hendrix and gone on to have very successful careers. We have had outstanding black athletes to come, only a few of whom received athletic scholarships before Hendrix stopped awarding scholarships based solely on athletic ability. Where my wife and I now live, three young, black women have worked in the dining room, all of whom went to Hendrix and later became medical doctors.

In the 1940s, I was pastor of a church in Little Rock and was on the city's Methodist Executive Committee with Lafayette Harris, president of Philander Smith College, and Roy Henderson. The three of us, with the strong leadership of Margaret Marshall, a Methodist deaconess, secured the property on which Camp Aldersgate was started. The money came from a $25,000 gift of the Women's Society of Christian Service, an organization of Methodists across the country. We agreed from the start that the camp would be open to blacks as well as whites. This brought much criticism from some of my church members and even my family. Some members from a nearby church threatened the building on the property.

Looking back on my ministry, I am especially proud of the fact that I had a part in opening up this premier liberal arts college to African American students, and that I helped establish Camp Aldersgate. I credit my understanding to The Methodist Church and its leadership, especially one lay couple in our church, Russell Henderson and his wife. They just felt it was the thing to do.

The Old Man and His Students:

The Wesley Foundation Years of A. W. Martin, Sr.

A. W. Martin, Jr.

A. W. Martin, Sr., one of the leading Methodist ministers in Arkansas in the mid-twentieth century, left his position as district superintendent of the Fort Smith district in 1945 to become Professor of Church Administration at the Perkins School of Theology at Southern Methodist University in Dallas. A compulsory retirement rule in 1957 forced his retirement there at age sixty-five, but church law permitted him to continue as a minister until he was seventy-two. So the bishop and cabinet, made up of the district superintendents in the North Arkansas Conference of The Methodist Church, faced an interesting problem: what to do with him? Dr. Roy Bagley, the superintendent of the Fayetteville District, came up with an ingenious suggestion: name him as minister to Methodist students at the University of Arkansas in Fayetteville as Director of the Wesley Foundation. This was an unusual suggestion, since the pattern of appointments at that time was almost invariably to name young men to student work.

Any question of Martin's ability to relate to college-age students was quickly answered as he and his wife Lloyd went about establishing a home away from home for students who needed a "surrogate parent or a safe place to drop in." Their small apartment behind the campus center meant that they were available at all hours. The center became the site for numerous social events, both scheduled and informal. Lloyd frequently had cookies, popcorn, and Rice-Krispie balls available. A grandfatherly type, he was a much safer counselor than a young man just out of seminary, and students felt secure in talking with him about their personal problems.

Martin liked to talk and enjoyed a good bull session as much as any college student. He could talk sports with the most avid fan, and he enjoyed an argument so much that he may even have dared on occasion to suggest the superiority of Southern Methodist Mustang football over the Razorbacks! He could talk farming and small-town life with

150

those who came from that kind of background and were having some problems adjusting to a large university campus. And of course he was willing to talk church with anyone anytime, combining a fierce loyalty with an equally sharp critique, as students struggled to come to terms with their relationship with an institution about which many of them were developing serious questions.

Even as he debated with students from time to time, he respected their opinions and heard them out. Their role as leaders in the work of the Wesley Foundation was crucial to his style of directing. A student who was at the university when the Martins arrived in 1957 remembered how Martin would let students talk "with all the wisdom and arrogance of nineteen or so years" but, at times, would remain silent, listening patiently to make them feel that their views deserved attention.

Martin's ability to see humor in life also facilitated his role of working with college students. His remarks were not always original, but they were almost always to the point. To persons who wanted to go slow on desegregation, he commented that it would not "be less painful for a dog to get its tail cut off one inch at a time." He once reminded a colleague regarding the struggle to end racism "that sometimes you have to get in a field with a bull, but you don't have to wear a red shirt when you do it."

A letter from Martin to students on the Wesley Foundation Council early in his second year at Fayetteville illustrates both his administrative skill and his understanding of what a full student program should include. Anticipating that meetings in Little Rock were going to prevent his attending a student council meeting, he wrote to his "friends and fellow workers" first to remind them about the need to plan for an upcoming open house and for chartering a bus to take members to a state Methodist Student Movement conference. He gave the students information about bus costs but left them with the question as to how much of the cost to cover from the regular budget and how much to ask individuals to pay.

From these scheduling matters he moved on to a concern about making their Foundation stronger, giving concrete suggestions for ways to make committees function better, since "the effectiveness of our program appears to rise or fall with the effectiveness of the several committees in our organization." The second half of the letter reminded the council of earlier discussions "about the need for a positive Christian witness…as we live our lives daily on the campus" and then stated his belief that students "more than any other group" were in a position to make an "effective witness of the Christian Gospel" in a time of "tensions over the racial situation in Arkansas." He concluded his letter, whose masthead identified him as director of the Foundation, with this personal challenge, now identifying himself as Minister to Students: "I…not only call upon you, the responsible officers and leaders of Wesley Foundation, but pledge myself to a deeper and more consistent devotion to the practical, day by day, opportunities presented in and through Wesley Foundation for witnessing for the faith that we profess."

Martin also brought to campus ministry his intelligence, intellectual curiosity, and mental alertness. Although a long way from his own seminary graduation, he had just spent over a decade on a university campus, where he was able to take advantage of public lectures in various fields of knowledge. And although his teaching was in the practical field, he had never been afraid to debate and discuss with his seminary colleagues who taught in the academic areas of Bible, church history, and theology. He had always had a special interest in Methodist history and was prepared to discuss anything related to the denomination at the drop of a hat. This kind of preparation, therefore, made him a natural in helping students plan the classes and forums of the Foundation program where they struggled to come to terms with the relevance of the Christian faith to life on a university campus. He was equally willing to invite guest speakers or discussion leaders on a variety of topics and to make presentations himself even if he had to do some crash research. He helped to create an atmosphere where students felt comfortable raising whatever questions came to mind.

One student remembered at the end of the Martins' tenure that the Wesley Foundation was "about the only place" students could "openly discuss religious, moral, and social matters, as well as events in the world situation." Another wrote to Martin about his "rare qualities of vitality and flexibility of thought….seldom found in youth, much less in your generation." A similar point was made by a student who wrote, "You have a tolerance for ideas; you are willing to examine new ideas honestly and accept or reject them according to their merit." Yet another recognized in him an ability "to communicate with people of various backgrounds and philosophies" that set him apart from his "previous experiences with ministers. The enigma for me is to explain how a man of the cloth of an older school of theology has been flexible enough to understand, accept, and communicate with this new generation...."

The realization that the church still had relevance to society, which many university students gained at the Wesley Foundation, happened in great measure to Martin's knowledge about and commitment to the church as it was, and a sense of what it could and should be. Even as he helped to shatter some naïve myths about the church, he responded to the idealism of youth with his own. In Arkansas in the late 1950s and early 1960s this meant, above all, directly confronting questions about race. Martin and his student colleagues in the Wesley Foundation participated in many activities to promote integration at the University of Arkansas and at other campuses statewide.

In 1960, at a state-level Methodist Student Movement Conference, the Wesley Foundation Council from the University of Arkansas recommended holding a future conference at Philander Smith College in Little Rock, a historically and predominantly black Methodist school. The recommendation was accepted. University of Arkansas Wesley Foundation students also voted in favor of a resolution, which passed, suggesting integration of all-white Hendrix College in Conway, the other Methodist school in the state.

A short time later, as a member of the Hendrix College Board of Trustees, Martin advised his colleagues that, as they approved continuing the segregated admissions policy "because that was what Methodists in Arkansas wanted," Methodist college youth of the state lean much more toward favoring integration than the Church constituency in general. The next year, a group of Methodist ministers went before Hendrix Board of Trustees to present a paper encouraging an open admissions policy at the college. A motion to accept the statement from the ministers was amended to include a promise to continue "vigorous Christian consideration of both the general question and the specific suggestions presented in the paper." Martin seconded the motion. Not until 1964 did the College officially revise its admission policy to include all qualified students regardless of race, color, or national origin.

Back on the University of Arkansas campus in April 1961, the Dean of Men and a group of students from Philander Smith spent a weekend as guests of the Wesley Foundation. They arrived on a

Saturday afternoon and participated in a "drop-in" party at the student center that night. On Sunday morning, they presented the program at the Forum Hour, participated in an informal discussion of current sit-in and kneel-in demonstrations, and then that evening told the "Philander Smith Story" at Central Methodist Church's Family Night.

For several years during Martin's tenure at the U of A, many Wesley Foundation members, who were also education majors, worked as assistants at the black Lincoln School in Fayetteville. As a result, children received more individual attention. One student remembered having parties at the school for the children, and there was also a dinner and talent show featuring students and community members at Central Methodist Church, which resulted in a swastika being painted on the front door of the university's Student Center. All of these efforts to build bridges across racial lines in Fayetteville are ones that Martin attended, supported, and allowed.

Racial concerns reached a confrontational level during the 1962-63 school year. In June 1962, Jim Loudermilk, a past student president of the Wesley Foundation, returned as its new associate director. He was even less patient with racism and the lack of progress at the university in this area than was Martin. As the handful of black students at the university found the United Methodist student center open to them, it was not long before they gathered there to plan an informational picket line/demonstration in front of the library about discriminatory housing policies. Loudermilk personally participated, and in recalling the event decades later, he remembered that a faculty member and dedicated Methodist layman was not pleased with the demonstration. Two days after the demonstration, Loudermilk and Martin found themselves in a meeting with Central Methodist Church's district superintendent, whom Loudermilk remembers questioned his level of maturity for university work, with the apparent implication that he should be given another appointment.

A short time later, under the influence of a small committee at Central Methodist Church that Martin referred to as "extremely conservative," both he and Loudermilk were facing a recommendation to the Wesley Foundation Personnel Committee that they not be returned, and that if they were, they be excluded from appearing in the pulpit of the church. The Foundation committee, at first, recommended that only Martin be allowed to continue for his last year before mandatory retirement set in, but then reversed itself by appointing Loudermilk Foundation director for the 1963-64 school year with Martin as his associate.

Noting that he and Jim had been working quietly and by persuasion for integration of public facilities in Fayetteville, Martin labeled their joint efforts as very modest activities on behalf of better relations between the races and blasted those who opposed them who thought that the Church exists to approve and make holy everything that our society does.

Martin gave his whole-hearted support as the Wesley Foundation Student Council maintained pressure on the university administration to integrate the school at all levels. The year before Martin's retirement, Wesley Foundation students continued to express their concern "that the principles and ideals of our Judeo-Christian heritage be brought to active expression in all relationships with our fellow students regardless of race or color." After noting that the university "had made commendable progress before the 1954 Supreme Court Decision on school integration...," they called attention to current discrimination in housing, athletics, admission procedures and use of the barber shop in the Student Union, asking the president and trustees "to eliminate...all semblance of discrimination based on race or color," and promised to support them in "practical expressions of true understanding and fair treatment of all persons...."

When Martin retired from his duties at the Wesley Foundation, he received many letters from current and former students commending him for staying the course. A former student wrote that "of all the factors that kept me interested, the most important was your aggressive, but scholarly, approach to the question of civil rights." Another said that the main thing she remembered was "the questions and discussions on race and different religions." The struggles over race were probably one of the things in mind when a student referred to Martin's "integrity in the midst of mendacity, your courage in the face of opposition, and your faith despite disillusioning experiences...." They were undoubtedly on the mind of another student, who, after noting Martin's ability to "keep up with and accept inevitable social changes," wrote, "You have the courage and audacity to say and do things that need to be said and done but are not popular with the public. Even though you are adept at smoothing over indignation, you have proven repeatedly that yours is not a ministry of public opinion."

Also on the occasion of his retirement, the state director for the Arkansas Methodist Student Movement acknowledged Martin for encouraging other ministers with students to be responsible leaders. He thanked Martin for his "prophetic statements and stands concerning Civil Rights" and for his role in "pushing and pulling the Methodist Student Movement into the intense struggle of being relevant both to the Gospel and to the college community."

Shortly after his death in 1973, the director of the Wesley Foundation at the University of Arkansas named Martin the modern pioneer in Wesley Foundation work in Arkansas. He said, "It was not just a matter of fund raising for all the foundations in the state. He was the real driving power behind the movement." Another, long-time Wesley Foundation director whose initial years coincided with Martin's, remembered the regular gatherings of the Foundation directors in Arkansas as times of debate and "talking together about anything and everything. Martin was always present, always vocal, and always willing to push his colleagues to witness for a cutting-edge position on race and war. He was our leader, and he set the tone for our work with students and faculty. He not only enriched our lives, he was instrumental in keeping most of us in The Methodist Church."

Editors' Note:

Much of the information and quotations used for this piece were gathered from friends, family, former students of A.W. Martin, and colleagues. Information was also obtained from 1960 issues of The Wesleyan *and* The Arkansas Traveler, *and a 1964 issue of* The Arkansas Methodist.

An Ever Increasing Battle
Ed Matthews

I was born and grew up in a section of Arkansas that had no African American population: Baxter, Izard, Stone, Marion, and surrounding counties. The few white, pioneer settlers, who might have owned slaves, didn't have them very long. The soil was thin and agriculture was little more than a sustenance-level activity. We never traveled much beyond our native region. I was too young to read the newspaper, we had no TV, and we listened to very little radio, as we had no electricity in my early childhood home in the 1930s and 1940s. As a result, I was never around blacks and knew very little about them.

I was embarrassingly naïve. As I studied the Civil War and the issue of slavery in school, I seemed to think that the problems were over and settled. I would come to find out that I knew very little about the issues.

An unusual thing happened one night when I was very young. A wholesale delivery truck out of Harrison, Arkansas, was traveling the rough, gravel Highway 5 by our home in the country. The truck broke down in front of our house just as it was getting dark; a wheel bearing on the rear axel had gone bad. There was no repairing it that night. Someone would have to go into Mountain Home to get a replacement bearing. The driver, traveling alone, was African American.

My parents took him into our home, fed him supper, and gave him a bed for the night. The next day, we assisted him with the repair, and the man went on his way. I felt it was strange that Daddy instructed us to tell no one about our befriending our overnight guest. Unbeknownst to me, it was a "code of the area" that "no black was to let the sun go down on him in those parts."

On another occasion, Daddy and I had gone into town one weekday. Daddy spotted a black man seated in an out-of-the-way place near Main Street eating his lunch from a sack. He was well dressed in a suit and tie. Daddy, our church's lay delegate to the Annual Conference, recognized this visitor as the current president of Philander Smith College, the black, Methodist-related college in Little Rock. Daddy asked him to go into the Hillbilly Café with him and eat a warm lunch, which he did.

Now, I thought that was very strange because I never saw my dad buy a restaurant-prepared meal anywhere, mostly because we didn't have the money. And here he was buying another man's meal! Only later did I realize that this college president, though dressed in a suit, would have been refused service if Daddy had not accompanied him inside. As a young child, I was unaware of the indirect conditioning I was receiving from my parents.

It was only as I graduated from high school in 1952 and entered the University of Arkansas at Fayetteville that I became suddenly and acutely aware of the injustices perpetrated on blacks at the hands of, and through policies and practices of, whites. At the university, I was very involved in Wesley Foundation, an organization for Methodist students. We had frequent programs and discussions that focused on racial issues. Increasingly, the media, by now there was TV, was reporting the growing racial tensions in the South. Then, in 1954, the Supreme Court decision came down. Suddenly, I was a citizen of a great big world with a heap of racial injustices going on all around me.

The university had black graduate students prior to 1954, but there were no black undergraduate students. That year, I was a head resident counselor for undergraduate men's housing on campus. The dormitory to which I was assigned was one of the first to be racially integrated. We were trained and instructed to hold many discussion sessions in the dorm, which we did. And things went extremely well.

By the end of the first semester of my third year at the university, the end of 1955, I realized that God was leaning on me rather heavily to consider using my life to address racial injustice more directly, perhaps even on a wider, global level. The Board of Missions of The United Methodist Church at that time had designed a missionary appeal program for the "Lands of Decision." Belgium Congo was one of those geographic areas. How prophetic the church's leadership was in focusing on those places around the globe that predictably could "blow up," become political hot spots, particularly as colonialism was thought to be coming to an end, as it did in Belgium Congo abruptly in June 1960.

I was hearing and reading much about conditions in Congo—politically, economically, and the history of Methodist missions there. I became particularly aware of the lack of attention the Belgians had given to agricultural development in their seventy-five year reign as colonialists in Africa. And it just so happened that agriculture was my field of academic studies. So, under what I felt was God's guidance, I sought approval from the Board of Missions to serve there. After graduating from the University of Arkansas, I completed seminary studies at Perkins School of Theology at Southern Methodist University and was ordained an elder by the North Arkansas Conference.

My wife, Pat Hunter Mathews, and I began our agriculture ministry in Belgium Congo in 1959. We lived and served in some very chaotic, politically tense days, when racial tensions internationally were at an all-time high. Many Belgians, and not a few missionaries, were killed. Those were the days of "ugly American, go home." It was in that setting that we experienced racial discrimination in reverse, and we just grew and grew and grew in our understanding of why people react as they so often do.

We served with more seasoned missionaries, what few returned after the mass evacuations following Congo's independence in June 1960. We lived and served in the Katanga Province in the southern third of Congo. Eleven days after the insistence by the Congolese nations that Congo be granted its political independence, our Katanga Province declared itself independent of the eleven-day-old Republique du Congo, under Moise Tshombe as president. Most of our colleagues supported the move, especially since Tshombe was Methodist. So, there was tension all around us!

When we returned to the United States following our four year assignment in Africa, I was investigated by the CIA due to possible Communist leanings. I learned we had been reported by some of our mission colleagues. Wow! The cause for racial justice took on a truly global perspective for my wife and me after serving in Africa, which has only increased to this day.

We returned to the United States in 1963-64, where we were assigned by the Board of Missions as "interpreters" of the struggle in Congo. The racial struggles in this country were far from over at that time, as well. We traveled around the country preaching and sharing with congregations, groups, schools, and civic clubs. We felt God using us to help others understand that He was calling everyone to reach out and build relationships with all of His people, at home and around the world.

159

In 1964, I entered pastoral ministry in Little Rock. Shortly after my first pastoral appointment, President John Kennedy was assassinated. Any pastor worth his or her salt felt called by God to speak out about the climate of the times that had made America so ripe for such tragic attitudes and actions. Arkansas Governor Orval Faubus took to the media to declare his innocence of doing anything that would contribute to such a climate. When I wrote him about such matters, he responded to my letter in the media. This made me particularly vulnerable when I participated in a sit-in at the state capitol in protest of its racial segregation policy. Some in leadership at the church I was serving called me on my stance. An overwhelming majority of the congregation stood with us and even those in opposition tolerated us.

I was enormously blessed to have served my next appointment with Dr. Robert E. L. Bearden at First Methodist Church in Little Rock, and my neighbor was Dr. Joel Cooper, pastor of Winfield Methodist. These two men stood like mighty oaks during those turbulent days of the 1960s. Later in the decade, I was appointed to Fordyce Methodist Church, a county seat with a large African American population. How beautifully the community accepted us, and we immediately felt part of it. There was a good working relationship between the two races here. The school superintendent was striving diligently to meet state and federal integration requirements, but had been unable to get a white teacher to teach in an all-black public school. In an emergency meeting of the school board called to address such a concern, I volunteered my wife Pat for the job. She was not currently teaching and her credentials had expired, but they saw to it that she was reaccredited and put to work! What an amazing story it is of how she won the hearts of the black community and the respect of the white community.

The Fordyce High School students worked long and hard at building a relationship between the races, as well. Early on, they elected as student body president an outstanding African American student. Many of the black students also were participating in ministry activities, much of which took place at the Methodist Church. But one Sunday, three of the black students who came to the Methodist Church for Sunday school stayed for worship. They were well-dressed and acted accordingly. That afternoon a meeting was called by some of the adult leadership in the church about it, mostly wanting my assurance that I had not invited them. It would have been more tolerable if the black students had just shown up on their own. I could only reply, "If you are asking if I specifically invited these three students to attend on this given Sunday, I did not. But if you are asking if everything I believe in and stand for invited them, then yes, I invited them." Relationships were edgy for a while, but we made it through.

In addition to the Fordyce Methodist Church, the community had a very strong African American Methodist Church. After its pastor's health failed, I was appointed as its interim pastor for several months until a permanent pastor could be appointed. I preached in that church each Sunday afternoon, worked with its leadership, visited its sick and conducted funerals as needed. This relationship was established at the invitation of that congregation's leadership and sanctioned by the leadership of the Fordyce Methodist Church. Pat and I felt as though the community as a whole respected what we worked for in Fordyce, for in our fifth year there, the Chamber of Commerce awarded me with the Outstanding Citizen award.

Now, in a retired relationship with the Arkansas Conference, how aware I am that through it all I was entirely too careful and cautious, perhaps taking the role of coward, consciously electing to be on the side of "keeping my pulpit" vs. being ridden out of town on the proverbial rail. How guilty I have felt as colleague after colleague took strong, prophetic stands while I stood by as a "reconciler" during my forty-five years of appointive ministry, forty-five years that paralleled the Civil Rights movement. Although retired as a pastor, I am still ready to work for peace and social justice, for indeed the battlefield is an ever increasing one.

The Burden of Silence
David McDonald

It was a beautiful, late summer day. Summer days in the South can be brutally hot and humid, but the dog days of summer had passed and the humidity level was finally tolerable. The pathway into the building was shaded with Bradford Pear trees lining the sidewalk. My parents had asked me to go with them as they looked at retirement homes. It was a bittersweet time. I was honored that they asked me to go with them, but a retirement home is where old people go, and old people eventually die. I wished my parents could be young again. As I watched them, my mind began to wander back to a time when they were young. I went back forty years to the 1960s. During those years, I saw my parents as the most courageous people I ever knew.

In the early 1960s, I was a teenager in the town of DeWitt, Arkansas. Some of my memories have dimmed, and I am sure there are the minor errors that invariably occur over decades, but I remember those times with a remarkable clarity. DeWitt was a small, south Arkansas town along the Mississippi River in an area referred to as the Grand Prairie. The rich, delta soil grew cotton in great quantities. Cotton generated old plantations and with that came slavery.

In the 1960s, slavery had been abolished for almost one-hundred years, but the foundation of the system was still very much in place. People were classified into one of two groups, black or white. We lived in a segregated system that was not only sanctioned by custom, but by a system of laws commonly called Jim Crow, which were designed to keep blacks and whites separate and very unequal. If these laws were not enough to enforce America's apartheid, organizations such as the Ku Klux Klan (KKK) would step in and impose Jim Crow by any means necessary.

Until I was eleven, I was only aware of segregation because it was discussed at home. The rules were so imbedded in our society that everyone played out their day-to-day roles without notice. In a town of about three thousand people, half were black and half were white. Segregation was like a fine oiled machine, all the moving parts operating in perfect sync. For whites, separation of the races appeared to take place easily and by mutual consent. But in reality, separation of the races took place by force. Tune-ups to the Jim Crow machine were brutal, but always took place out of the sight of white people.

My parents opposed segregation and that was the reason they talked about it with us at home. There was a lot of talk about blacks among my peers, but it wasn't about the rules of segregation. It was about blacks being inferior and the racial slurs. The word nigger was everywhere. It was used in the name of foods, in phrases and slang terms, and it was peppered throughout the sayings of the day.

My first Jim Crow memory was when I went to the hardware store for my mother. After I gathered the things on the list, I moved to the end of the line of customers waiting to pay for their goods. When I reached the line, everyone stepped aside and allowed me to go first. I was confused when the clerk told me that I should step forward and pay. I told the clerk that there are people ahead of me, but he said, "They'll wait, you can go first." On the way home, I marveled at how nice the adults were to let me go first.

When I reached home, I told my mother what had happened. She asked me if the people in front of me were black, and I told her they were. With a look of disgust and in an angry voice, Mother said, "Because you are white and they are Negroes, they had to let you go first. That is the way it is, and it's wrong." That was the first time I remember seeing the finely oiled Jim Crow machine. I was coming of age.

To have this conversation with my mother in a white, southern home in 1961 was an amazing event. I was the only one I knew of who lived in a home where you could not say the word nigger. I was taught it was a terrible word. My parents told us that being called a nigger lover was a good thing because it meant that we were treating all people as human beings. If we could do that, we were being good Christians and good people.

Money was not in great supply in DeWitt, but I was given an allowance of seventy-five cents each week. I was required to save twenty-five cents and give twenty-five cents to the church, which left me with only twenty-five cents for my own use. If I wanted to get anything other than an occasional Coke, I had to come up with another source of income. On one occasion, I noticed a large number of Coke bottles in our neighbor's back yard trash barrel. Bottles could be redeemed for two cents each, and with my finely honed math skills, I easily calculated that a dozen bottles would be only one cent short of doubling my disposable income.

Our neighbor was a wealthy and bigoted woman. And I didn't know that she and my mother had recently had a falling out when my mother told her she didn't agree with her racial views. A black man worked for our neighbor. He was referred to only as "my house nigger" or "monkey," which explains the way he was treated. One day I noticed him in the yard and ran over to see if I could collect the bottles. A look of panic came across his face. He quickly looked down to avoid eye contact with me and would not face me directly. He said that if he were to give me the bottles, he could lose his job. Even as a child, I understood this event. This man was terrified of what could happen to him if he were to give me a few Coke bottles that were going to be thrown away. His employer had complete control of this man's destiny due only to the color of his skin. I never learned this man's name.

I was beginning to understand Jim Crow and with increasing frequency. What had seemed like a finely oiled machine was beginning to turn hideous. Being an early teen, I wanted so much to fit in, and, for the most part, I did. But there were times that I understood I wasn't like the others. My father told me about the following event. I remember it because it happened at one of my friend's homes. A black man had unintentionally gone to the side door of my friend's house. A black person was always to go to the back door. His father answered the door to find the black man standing there and flew into a rage. He stormed out of the house, hitting the man, knocking him down. Cursing and yelling, he went back into the house to get a gun. Fortunately, the black man was able to run away, but if my friend's father had succeeded in killing the man, there would have been no serious consequences.

In the Arkansas of 1963, it was too dangerous for blacks to speak out in favor of civil rights. My peers would frequently tell me how their parents had asked their black servants what they thought of civil rights, or desegregation, as it was called then. The answer was always the same, "You treat me and my family good. I don't like this desegregation, it ain't right. We like to be to ourselves." Blacks who answered this way, and they all did, were referred to as "good niggers."

On Friday, November 22, 1963, John Kennedy was shot and killed in Dallas, Texas. For all of us that experienced this event, it is engraved in our memories with remarkable clarity. When the announcement was made on the school intercom, one of my brothers was in a class that cheered. When class ended, everyone made their way to the hall where I heard someone shout, "They finally got that nigger lover." Thirteen-year-old boys don't cry, but it was all I could do to keep from breaking down until I got home. I thought I was the only one of my friends who believed what had happened was a terrible thing.

I remember Sunday, November 24, 1963, as being clear and cool. In times of crisis, the rural South often turns to their faith. So on that Sunday, the churches were filled. Daddy was the minister of the Methodist Church and for several years, he had been preaching against segregation, but the sermon references were always subtle. That Sunday, the title of the sermon was "It is Hate that Kills," and it spoke directly to segregation and racial bigotry.

Daddy quoted a newspaper editorial, "Innocent children have been dynamited in Sunday school. We have grown used to seeing on television and in news pictures the hate-twisted faces of young men and women, as well as adults crying out the most violent threats and expressing a virulence of venom against their country and its authority. So, at this hour, before we begin to mourn, we would do well to understand that hate can kill a president, and, if unchecked on behalf of morality, decency and human dignity, it can kill a nation or so weaken it that it will die."

My father then said, "Who killed the president? I suppose you could say we all are part of the slaying. I helped kill the president when I did not and do not speak out against hate. The racial problems that confront us are stirred up by hate. Hate will not solve any problem, much less the problem of living together as brothers." The burden of silence had become too great a burden for my father, and the message of the sermon could not be overlooked.

At an official board meeting the next February, it was proposed that if a black person was to come into the church, he or she would not be seated, but directed to the nearby black church. It was no coincidence that this resolution was introduced on the date designated in the Methodist Church as Race Relations Sunday. In the discussion that ensued, it became apparent that should the resolution pass, my father, as pastor, could and would overrule it. To avoid the division that was about to take place, the resolution was tabled until the following month. That night my parents gathered the entire family around the kitchen table. They told us what had happened and explained that because of the conflict there might be problems. Luckily, the resolution never made it back to the floor at the next board meeting. And some members never returned, either.

Even with the resolution out of the picture, the issue of blacks attending church was not over. My father immediately took steps to assure that no one would be turned away. He went to each of the ushers and asked if they would be willing to seat a black person. If he was not, he was very tactfully replaced. All the ushers were told that if a black person was to attend a service, he or she should be seated with my father's family. This was no small issue. Seating a black person with a white family would be breaking one more of society's rules. But we were never to know how the congregation would react. My father was appointed to another church before we had the occasion to seat a black family.

On Sunday, May 24, the church service began like any other. When the time came for the sermon, my father announced that he had been reappointed to DeWitt, and that he believed it was time to address some issues he saw as central to the church's future. He spoke of his belief that Christianity was a faith rooted in love and about his conviction that Christianity was an inclusive faith, not an exclusive faith. He went on to say that those in the sanctuary were in a sacred place, and that all who wished to attend must always be welcomed, without regard to race. Several times he repeated his belief that Jesus would welcome all people into any place of worship.

My father's profound belief that the church was for all people was the theme throughout the service that day. I have since looked at the sermon notes, and, to me, the words sound mild to today's standards, but in south Arkansas in 1964, the words were enormously powerful. I was listening to my father say things that had never been said from the pulpit in a church in DeWitt. I had frequently sat in Sunday school classes and listened to teachers and peers justify bigotry from Biblical passages, but now it was being said from the pulpit that not only was bigotry wrong, it was not sanctioned in this church.

When the sermon ended, my father looked out at the congregation and did something he had not planned. He simply told the congregation it was dismissed and walked out. There was no closing prayer, song, or benediction. In over forty-five years as a minister, he had never walked out of a service. People sat in their pews stunned and confused. It seemed like an eternity before people began to leave. Few spoke. Everyone just went to their cars and drove away.

My brother rushed back to Daddy's office to see him supporting himself against his desk. He saw the board member who had supported Daddy at the board meeting talking with him. Later, as an adult, my brother asked Daddy what he was thinking at that moment. He said he was terrified. I never knew that about my father. To me, he was the most courageous person I knew. My father took a public stand for basic human dignity that was based on his strong religious faith, which has continued to shape me and my brothers long into adulthood.

The minister that followed my father at DeWitt did not share his views on racial equality. The church did not have anyone to preach the gospel of inclusion, and no black person ever came to the church. It seemed that what happened the Sunday of my father's stand was meaningless to everyone but my family.

In 1995, I was attending a conference in which I was to introduce the keynote speaker, Carol Hampton Rasco, President Clinton's domestic policy advisor and DeWitt native. Before her speech, we talked about what had happened in DeWitt as we were growing up there. When she took the podium, she told about my father and the stand he took at the church that Sunday. She said her belief in social justice came from her family, her church, and my father. What seemed like minor and largely meaningless gestures in 1963 and 1964 ended up having an effect in the White House thirty years later. DeWitt did have meaning, and has shown us that sometimes the safety of silence is too great a burden to bear.

Small Increments of Justice
John Miles

After graduation from Perkins School of Theology in 1954, I was assigned to Wilmot, Arkansas, deep in the Delta South, just north of Louisiana and west of Mississippi. Wilmot was a town of about 750, with approximately 450 African Americans and 300 European-Americans. There was much tension in the area due to the Supreme Court's recent *Brown v. Board of Education* ruling. The Civil Rights issue was on everyone's minds.

On Christmas Eve in 1956, I was downtown in Wilmot. The streets were crowded with people shopping and visiting. All of a sudden, there was a commotion in front of a store. I noticed a group of young, white people pouring out of the pool hall with their pool cues. The African Americans all around me were grabbing ax handles that were on display at the hardware store. I pushed through the crowd as a young neighbor of mine shouted to me, "Merry Christmas, preacher" and went on by.

Lying on the sidewalk, covered in blood, was a young African American whom I also knew. I got between the two groups, trying to quiet them and find out what had happened. I learned that my young neighbor had come out of the pool hall in a hurry, smelling like a distillery, and the young black man was passing by with boxes of toys for his children's Christmas. The white man knocked him down kicked him, then stomped the presents. The victim's teeth were ruined.

I told the white men to go. They let me know in no uncertain terms that no white man had ever been punished by the law for abusing a black person in that area. I swore before God and all that I held sacred that things would change in Wilmot. When the crowd dispersed, I went to every business in the small town and told them what I was doing and why. I called the mayor, the constable, the city council members, and we got a warrant for the white man's arrest. He was arrested that very night. Though he was released on bond, he was found guilty of assault at a trial. Through conversation and compromise, we set a new pattern for justice in that small corner of Arkansas.

Most members of the church supported me in this or I could not have gotten it done. When I got to the small country church Christmas Sunday morning, I was told by the young men who worked with the accused that if I went into the pulpit to preach they would pull me out and do violence to various parts of my body. So, instead of preaching, I pulled up a chair in the aisle and began a dialogue with them. They did not leave, nor did they hit me, but it was never the same in that small church. It is the price you pay for trying to be faithful.

Similar things were happening all over the delta. Some ministers paid a horrible price, but they were faithful, and by and large, most of the Methodist ministers in that period of time were able to work for small increments of justice. As I look back, I see how much we should have done and how much there is left to do.

Philander Smith College: The Untold Story Behind the Civil Rights Movement
N. J. Murray-Norman

The Little Rock Central High School crisis has become synonymous with the Civil Rights movement. So synonymous that if you Google *Little Rock* or even the words *civil rights*, Little Rock Central High constantly pops up. Not taking anything away from this great incident in the tapestry of the Civil Rights movement, the story to dismantle Jim Crow in the local businesses of Little Rock is often overlooked. Whenever one thinks of sit-ins, places like Greensboro, North Carolina, come to mind. If one were to mention freedom rides, Congress of Racial Equality (CORE) and Student Nonviolent Coordinating Committee (SNCC), places such as Memphis, Nashville, Georgia, Alabama, and Mississippi come to mind, not Little Rock. Had the Little Rock Central High School crisis not taken place, would there have been enough momentum to continue the Civil Rights struggle to end segregation in Little Rock?

Both events are important in understanding what impact Little Rock had on the Civil Rights movement. In trying to research and fully assess the impact of the movement to end segregation, very little information could be found about Philander Smith College students and the role they played in ending Jim Crow in Little Rock.

Philander Smith College, a United Methodist-related institution, was founded in 1877 to educate former African American slaves.[1] From the founding of the college in 1877 through 1960, faculty, staff, and students had been actively involved in the struggle to end segregation and to shatter the stereotypes whites may have had of African American students. While this battle may have taken place in the classroom and even in other private settings, far away from the scope of public attention, momentum was building to end segregation and to advance the Civil Rights movement publicly.

Two white professors, Georg Iggers and Lee Lorch, who worked at Philander Smith College during the early 1950s, were active in the National Association for the Advancement of Colored People (NAACP).[2] Iggers and Lorch sat on the Little Rock NAACP Executive Committee, which was one of many organizations instrumental in helping organize the desegregation plan of the Little Rock public schools. Iggers' involvement with the NAACP no doubt sparked a fire in those working in and attending Philander Smith College.

Iggers, a German Jew, fled to America from the Nazis in 1938. While attending college in Richmond, Virginia, he became actively involved in inter-racial groups who were working to promote a better understanding of the races in the South. He moved to Little Rock with his wife in 1950 and taught at Philander Smith College until 1956. He was active with the Little Rock chapter of the NAACP from his arrival in 1950 until he departed to Louisiana in 1956.[3] Following the departure of Iggers, Lorch and his wife Grace remained active in the NAACP. The catalysts for the sit-ins during the Little Rock Central High event were in part due to the involvement of Philander Smith College alumni, faculty, and students.

Following the integration of Little Rock Central High, student-led activist groups were gaining momentum in the South. Groups such as CORE and SNCC had made their way to Little Rock. These organizations were responsible for helping dismantle Jim Crow laws not just in Little Rock, but throughout the South. The sit-ins that took place in downtown Little Rock were inspired by the sit-in incidents that took place in Greensboro, North Carolina.

Four black students from North Carolina Agricultural and Technical College were the first to ask for service at the "whites only" counter of a downtown Greensboro Woolworth store on February 1, 1960.[4] This event was the first of many student-led, nonviolent events that spread throughout the South. While the demonstrators themselves advocated nonviolence, it was those who disagreed with the demonstrators who often reacted with violence. SNCC and CORE coordinators taught students to use methods of nonviolence inspired by Mohandas K. Gandhi.[5] The essence of SNCC and CORE was to protest without the use of violence, either physical or verbal.

The success of the sit-ins in Greensboro is reflected by support the students received from the African American community. The success in Greensboro stemmed not only from the student led organizations, but also from the support of church leaders, businessmen, and other groups such as the NAACP and the Southern Christian Leadership Conference (SCLC).[6] Student-led organizations were often supported, in numbers and financially, by patrons of various public sectors.[7]

The sit-ins at Little Rock were not as welcomed and were not readily supported by the African American community. With the support received by others during the integration of Little Rock Central High, Philander Smith College had taken a backlash. The two Philander Smith professors involved in the desegregation plan of the Little Rock school district had received threats that endangered their lives and the lives of their families. Support from the college president, Dr. M. Lafayette Harris, was minimal. In an interview given to the *Arkansas Democrat* in March 1960, Dr. Harris told the paper that the college would never subscribe to mass action. Philander Smith College students were told not to go downtown. They were restricted from attending any off-campus activity that would beget negative attention to the college.

During that time, the NAACP and Philander Smith student leaders planned a boycott of Little Rock's white-owned businesses, such as Woolworth, S. S. Kresge, S. H. Kress, and W. T. Grant, because of their consistent public declaration of segregation. These first attempts at public sit-ins failed dismally due to the African American community's lack of support. Coordination and cooperation between existing leaders and organizations were not in place and could not be mobilized. In absence of the necessary infrastructure, fines and sentences grounded the movement.[8]

On March 10, 1960, fifty Philander Smith College students protested against segregated lunch counters at the downtown F. W. Woolworth. The officials at Woolworth refused to serve the students and immediately alerted Chief of Police Eugene Smith.[9] By the time the police arrived only five students remained at the counter. These students were Charles Parker, Frank James, Vernon Mott, Eldridge Davis, and Chester Briggs. Following the arrest of these five students, the Little Rock NAACP posted bail for the young men at $100 each.

The response from the white community spread with much condemnation. The African American community's reaction to the protest was mixed. While some supported the students in their endeavors, others frowned upon their actions. Among those was Philander Smith College President Dr. Harris[10] Despite Harris' opposition to the demonstrations of the previous students, other students such as Frank James Lupper, Thomas Robinson, Sammy Baker, Winston Jones, McLoyd Buchanan, William Rogers, Jr., Melvin T. Jackson, and Eugene D. Smith were also arrested for their involvement in sit-ins at department stores such as Blass and Pfieffer.[11] They were fined and sentenced to sixty days in jail. Following their appeals to the Pulaski County Circuit Court, their fines were doubled with a sixty day jail sentence.[12]

Due to Philander Smith's summer recess, the sit-ins once again came to a halt. During the fall semester of 1960, students were organized by Arkansas SNCC coordinator Reverend William E. Bush of Toledo, Ohio, and Frank James, who was arrested for involvement in prior student-led sit-ins, served as its executive secretary. Dr. Harris was no longer serving as president of Philander Smith College, and with his absence, the organization gradually gained momentum. However, the African American community as a whole still was not supporting public sit-ins. Without the support from the wider African American community, efforts to extend the sit-ins to a boycott of stores would be futile.[13] According to reports from the Arkansas Council on Human Relations (ACHR), they too lamented concerns for the lack of coordinated support from the adult community which was showing its usual fragmentation and divisiveness.[14] Without this support, the movement to dismantle Jim Crow in local businesses failed.

The sit-ins were the first of many tactile approaches aimed at ending segregation in local businesses in Little Rock. Following the sit-ins and freedom rides of CORE and SNCC members, local groups began to form coalitions to dismantle Jim Crow in white-owned businesses that exclusively served whites. Without the initial efforts of Philander Smith College students, the dismantling of Jim Crow would have been even more tumultuous.

End Notes

1. 2005-2007 *Philander Smith College Catalog*, 1

2. John A. Kirk, *Redefining the Color Line: Black Activism in Little Rock, Arkansas, 1940-1970*, 90

3. Ibid, 92

4. Ibid, 141

5. Teachings of Mohandas Ghandi

6. Aldon D. Morris, *The Origins of the Civil Rights Movement: Black Communities Organizing for Change*, 196

7. Ibid, 196-198

8. *Arkansas Council on Human Relations Quarterly Report*, January-March 1960

9. *Arkansas Democrat*, March 10, 1960, *Arkansas Gazette*, March 11, 1960

10. *Arkansas Democrat*, March 13, 1960

11. *Arkansas Democrat* April 13, 1960

12. *Arkansas Democrat*, June 17, 18, 1960

13. *Arkansas Council on Human Relations Quarterly Report*, October-November, 1960

14. Memorandum, Little Rock ACHR to SRC, December 6, 1960, reel 141, frame 0218, SRC Papers, Library of Congress, microfilm.

Integration at Hoxie, Arkansas
Ken Parker

In the fall of 1955, two years before Little Rock Central High School was catapulted onto front pages around the world, the public school board in Hoxie, Arkansas, made history, and its attorneys established legal precedent.

Hoxie was a farming community at the junction of the Missouri Pacific and Frisco Railroads. Its school district, strapped for funds, nevertheless maintained the legally required "separate but equal" school for black pupils in the first through eighth grades and transported black high school pupils to an all-black school at Jonesboro. The separate school for Negroes was hardly equal, however. It was a deteriorating building with an outdoor toilet.

The Fayetteville and Charleston school districts, which had few black pupils, stopped their transportation costs by quietly integrating the black pupils into the previously all-white schools. This was done with little fanfare. In fact, there was no announcement to the outside world that Charleston schools would be integrated, and residents of the district refused to discuss it with outsiders.

Hoxie was a slightly different case. For one thing, it was a delta farming community. For another, like many school districts in the rural South, it operated with a "split term." School started in July and recessed in the fall to allow pupils to help pick cotton, resuming when all the cotton had gone to the gins.

The Hoxie School Board, encouraged by the superintendent of schools, Kunkel Edward Vance, decided by unanimous vote to desegregate. Superintendent Vance later stated that this was done because it was right in the sight of God, it complied with the ruling of the United States Supreme Court, and it would save money for the district.

The district made no special preparations for the school term, and all facilities of the school were integrated, including rest rooms, cafeterias and drinking fountains. School opened with no incidents. There were twenty-one black students and one thousand white students. At

175

first, black and white students stayed in separate groups, but that ended soon as white students began to ask black students to join in basketball games and other activities.

On July 25, 1955, two weeks after the uneventful opening of school, *Life* magazine had a major article entitled "Integration at Work in Hoxie," and it included pictures of black and white students sitting together in classes and playing together on the school grounds. With this attention, Hoxie—because of its split term and probably one of the only integrated schools in the 1955 South—became a focal point for white supremacists across the country. Hoxie residents started receiving mail from distant places urging them to resist integration.

Thus inspired, about three hundred and fifty residents attended a meeting on August 3 to organize and protest desegregation of the schools. The group called themselves the Hoxie Committee for Segregation and asked the school board to reconsider its action, which it refused to do. The committee called for a boycott and said that the absentee rate as a result was fifty percent. The school superintendent refused to announce the number of students absent but said it was less than fifty percent.

The school board's attorney, Methodist Sunday school teacher Bill Penix of Jonesboro, who was joined by his partners, his wife Marian and his father Roy, and later by Little Rock attorney Edwin E. Dunaway, filed suit against the protesters. Penix said it was Marian's idea on the ground that, since the Supreme Court had ordered desegregation of schools, the federal government had a correlative duty to defend the school board's actions in complying with that order. It was a theory that had not been tested.

A petition was filed in United States District Court for the Eastern District of Arkansas. It sought an injunction against Herbert Brewer and the Hoxie Committee for Segregation; Little Rock attorney Amis Guthridge; White America, Inc.; state Senator James D. Johnson of Crossett; Curt Copeland of Hot Springs, who published a white supremacy newspaper; and the White Citizens Council of Arkansas. Guthridge, Johnson and Copeland had spoken at a rally on the courthouse square at Walnut Ridge and had lent counsel to the segregationist group. The petition maintained that the federal government owed protection to the school board in carrying out its duties as outlined by the Supreme Court.

On November 1, 1955, Judge Thomas C. Trimble granted a preliminary injunction, ruling that his court had jurisdiction over the matter and declared that the 1954 Supreme Court decision had nullified Arkansas state laws mandating segregation in public schools. Judge Trimble said that the defendants in the case had planned and conspired to prevent desegregation of the Hoxie schools. He set a hearing for December 8 at Jonesboro and said a special judge would hear the petition for a permanent injunction.

The Penixes and Dunaway were sad-hearted when they learned that the case would be heard by Judge Albert L. Reeves of Kansas City. They did not know anything about Judge Reeves, except that he had taken senior judge status. A quick check of Who's Who in America revealed that he was eighty-two years old, a Republican and had been appointed to the bench by President Warren G. Harding. The lawyers doubted he would have liberal leanings.

What they didn't know about until later was Judge Reeves' devotion to the rule of law. January 9, 1956, he ruled that Arkansas's school segregation laws were nullified, that the school board was acting within the law when it voted to desegregate the schools, and that the board members, having determined that integration was practical, would have been subject to severe civil and criminal penalties had they backed down. He made the injunction permanent and noted that it applied not only to the defendants but to all persons having knowledge of it.

Judge Reeves' decision was appealed to the United States Court of Appeals for the Eighth Circuit, and the United States Justice Department entered pleadings siding with the school board, the first time the department had intervened to assist a school board in obeying the principles of Brown v. Board of Education. The State of Georgia filed a brief supporting the segregationists' stand. The Court of Appeals upheld Judge Reeves in an opinion which set the legal precedent that the federal government had a correlative duty to uphold school boards which attempted to abide by the Supreme Court's decision in the Brown case.

Superintendent Vance and school board members were subjected to harassment at the hands of the segregationists. But they stuck to their guns. Also subjected to the harassment was Reverend H. L. "Pop" Robison, pastor of Hoxie Methodist Church. On the eve of the school's opening day in July 1955, Rev. Robison had urged the young people in his congregation to go to school the next day and treat minority students as they would want to be treated if they were in the minority. He also urged parents of students, whatever their opinions, to refrain from discussing them in front of their children.

As a result of this stand, the pastor's sleep was interrupted by automobile horns being sounded in front of the parsonage throughout the night and individuals crawling under the house and hammering on the floor. Rev. Robison's mother lived with her bachelor son. She volunteered to answer the phone at the parsonage. There would be a call for her son, and she would say he was not in and ask if she could take a message. That would be followed by an outburst of profanity, racial slurs and threats, to which Mrs. Robison—acting as though she were a dithering old lady—would say, "Oh, Pop will be so sorry he missed your call!"

Pop Robison had the backing of his district superintendent Reverend Elmo Thomason and a Roman Catholic priest at neighboring Walnut Ridge. These were the principal clerical voices supporting the school board. At least one Missionary Baptist minister was quoted as telling his congregation that God would send ruin on Hoxie for daring to mix the races.

The Little Rock Central High School crisis came two years later, and until his death, Bill Penix maintained that, had the Little Rock School Board followed the course the Hoxie School Board took, there would have been no crisis.

Editors' Note:
   Ken Parker recorded these events while he was the State Editor for the Arkansas Gazette.

An Arkansas Pastor's Memories
Bob Sessions

My first appointment after seminary was as pastor to St. John's Methodist Church in Van Buren and another small, rural church nearby. One Sunday after preaching at the smaller church, one of its members asked me to his home for dinner. As we sat on his porch in rocking chairs, "the women folks" prepared dinner in the kitchen. He knew I had supported desegregation of public schools, not only in the pulpit, but also in civic clubs and many formal and informal groups. I knew that all of that was on the mind of my host, although he did not mention it, as we rocked on his porch that Sunday afternoon. Then, suddenly, he came out with his thoughts. "You know, Brother Bob, it's hard for a feller to get away from his rearin'."

Many sincere Christians and non-Christians in and around Van Buren had to get away from, or beyond, their rearin' following the Supreme Court's decision. One of the highlights of that time for me, was when the president of our church youth group, Angie Evans, a high school senior and president of the high school's Student Council, stood in a mass meeting at the high school and told those who were protesting desegregation that if they would trust the students, faculty, and school board, the desegregation problems could be worked through in a Christian and American way. Angie's words proved to be the turning point of that meeting and the beginning of a sensible, although not always easy, change to a desegregated school system.

It was not easy or popular in those years for a pastor to speak out in favor of brotherhood, much less for desegregation, and even for true equality for all Americans in personal and public life. I remember very vividly a good friend in Van Buren saying to me, "Bob, one of these mornings they're going to drag your dead body out of the Arkansas River all covered with chains and locks and heavy weights, and they are going to say, 'You know, Bob should have had enough sense to know not to try to swim that river with all those weights on him!'"

179

After Van Buren, I served six years as pastor of the First Methodist Church in Booneville. I tried to work in the North Arkansas Conference not only for progress in race relations, but also for what I saw as the many needs within the conference, state, and nation on social issues. While there, I wrote an article, "Are Southern Ministers Failing the South," which was published by *The Saturday Evening Post*. I said we were. One of our church lay leaders, along with others on the front steps of the church, wanted to be in a prominent position in the picture for the magazine. But later, when he heard the picture was to be used in an article favoring desegregation, he came and asked me to request that his figure be cut out of the printed picture. *The Post* ultimately used an integrated group on the front steps of a large Methodist church in Fort Smith, Arkansas, thirty-five miles away.

I left Arkansas, saddened emotionally by leaving, but challenged intellectually, to pursue a doctoral degree at Boston University and a life as a pastor and administrator in higher education. But I have never lost my love for my home state, its churches, and especially its people.

Bringing People Together
C. Ray Tribble

Camp Aldersgate in Little Rock, Arkansas, a nonprofit organization of the General Board of Global Ministries of The United Methodist Church, has a long and successful history, as you will read below. Nearly sixty years old, its mission today is the same as it was in 1947, to encourage social justice, racial harmony, and provide life enrichment opportunities for all in a natural setting.

Its name was suggested by Reverend Harry Bass, a black pastor, because of its association with John Wesley, the founder of Methodism. Wesley related how he went to a meeting on Aldersgate Street in London in 1738 and upon hearing a reading from Martin Luther's preface to the book of Romans, he felt his heart "strangely warmed" by the Holy Spirit. Reverend Bass remarked that he, too, felt his heart warmed every time he entered the grounds of the camp, and he hoped all who visited it would share this experience and would be inspired to go forth to serve their church and communities.

A central part of the Aldersgate story belongs to Margaret Marshall, a deaconess in the Methodist Church. After serving in many areas of service, she was sent to Little Rock in 1943 to direct the City Mission Board, now the Little Rock Methodist Council, which had begun programs of all types in both black and white Methodist churches. Its members were made up of women from local churches and the community. The programs in Little Rock flourished as Marshall worked with many volunteers. The success of Marshall's inter-racial programs was rewarded with a $25,000 grant. The question then was how best to use the money?

Marshall conceived the idea for a Methodist camp open to all people of all ages and to all types of groups, organizations, and associations. It would be in a natural setting so as to encourage positive interaction without the pressures and stigmas of the outside world. It would be the first place in the South where inter-racial groups could work together on the basis of equality and brotherhood. As search groups were sent out

181

around Little Rock to find the ideal location for the new camp, Marshall remembers that it enabled her to experience some of the hardships blacks faced when it came to finding cafes that would serve them food.

In 1946, an advertisement was found for the Windy Willow Turkey Farm. The 120-acre property was for sale and was only about four miles out of the city limits. Those who visited the farm described it as "a rough, thinly populated area, pretty well abandoned; a dismal sight." But there was potential. Six structures on the property could be renovated relatively quickly, and the land had a constant water supply from a number of natural springs. The utilities were in place, and there was the possibility of building a lake at minimal expense. Marshall, away at the time, received a telegram, "Hurry home. Your child is about to be born."

As you might expect, however, not all Methodists were pleased with the idea of promoting race relations. But fortunately, a very vocal group of young people and adults could hardly wait for the camp to become a reality. In only four months of hard work, the camp had been renovated enough to house its first campers. What a wonderful way for people of all ages, races, and stations to come together and know each other. Camp Aldersgate was dedicated in June 1947, and "the place began to jump with joy" as many of the camp's activities were promoted throughout the area.

One of the first activities held at Aldersgate was a conference for the Woman's Society of Christian Service. Three Arkansas Conferences were involved: the Little Rock and North Arkansas Conferences were all white and the Southwest Conference was black. Women from all three came. The program was planned with skill and challenge to bring the participants into the very presence of God. In the last session, the Holy Spirit took over and woman after woman rose to tell what God had done for her through this meeting together.

Youth groups were among the first visitors at the camp. One young person, Bill Holmes, liked the camp so much he asked for a summer job there. Bill was a fine young fellow who had not only had a real conversion experience, but was a volunteer for the ministry. Bill said, "I can be a janitor, I can be a life saver, I can help you with any problems you may have." He came to work with us, and I know we couldn't have functioned without him. He succeeded as a minister, for many years serving as the senior pastor of Metropolitan Memorial United Methodist

Church in Washington, D.C. This is just one of the young people who visited us at the camp who later became ministers.

Not long after Aldersgate opened, a black Presbyterian minister brought his youth for a week-long retreat. One night he had vespers near the camp entrance. During the service, an elderly white man from a nearby house joined them in their service. He was welcomed. The black minister later told Miss Marshall that "if you Methodists have lighted the fire, surely, we can add fuel."

There were difficult times, as well. On one occasion, some football players from Philander Smith, a black, Methodist college in Little Rock, were attending the camp. One evening, huge flashlights appeared all over the grounds. Needless to say, the boys left and never returned. Then on another occasion, the dam in the lake was blown away by dynamite, draining out all the water. The camp wasn't too damaged, but it made us remember that not everyone was happy about the concept of Camp Aldersgate.

As the first few months of the camp's existence came and went, everyone realized that it needed a director. Margaret Marshall agreed to serve as an interim director until a permanent one could be hired. In 1949, Reverend Robert McCammon was selected as its first full-time director. After accepting a pastoral appointment in 1950, McCammon turned over the position to Milam Ware Willis, "Mike." Mike, his wife Verna, and their seven-year-old son Michael made Camp Aldersgate their home until 1962.

The climate in Little Rock during Mike's tenure as camp director reflected that of the nation. Interest focused more and more on racial segregation. The Methodist Churches were not sheltered from this climate, and certainly neither was Camp Aldersgate. In the first few years of the 1950s, Mike began building on the summer programs already in existence. Even though much was being accomplished, these were times when the divisive faces of prejudice, hatred, greed, selfishness, and secularism threatened the life of the church and Aldersgate. Those associated with the camp received hate letters throughout the 1950s and 1960s. And as mentioned above, property at the camp was damaged on more than one occasion.

Despite this, great things were happening there. Many lay people and clergy in the Methodist Church were encouraging the use of Camp

Aldersgate and provided leadership in many of the events. It had indeed become an important location for inter-racial groups to meet and discuss. One of those meetings took place in March 1956 when the Arkansas Council on Human Relations met to discuss strategies for increasing voter registration and for filing lawsuits in desegregation cases. This brought Aldersgate public attention as a setting for grass-roots activism in the cause for integration and human rights. Fortunately, this led to integrated meetings between parents and teachers in Little Rock's Central High School crisis. Even though progress was being made at the camp on this issue, participants received harassing phone calls and letters. The state police monitored those who entered and exited the camp by taking car license plate numbers.

In spite of these negative events, Mike and his family say they never lost their love for Aldersgate and never stopped working for its growth. Mike reflects that "growth" is exactly what happened there; growth not only in the camp itself, but also deep, personal growth for him and his family and most of those who had the wonderful opportunity to spend time there.

When Mike and Verna left in 1962, I took over as camp director. Mike and I had met some years earlier, and he remembered my interest in furthering race relations through church-sponsored projects. This interest began in the cotton fields of my youth when I helped my family and others, black and white, pick cotton in the summer and frequently would visit others' homes. It continued into my adulthood as my wife and I worked with the Alabama Housing Authority, which administered federal, low-income housing. Our job was to visit the families who had applied for the housing. We witnessed poverty-stricken areas where disease, malnutrition, illiteracy, and ignorance were rampant. So many children seemed without loving care. This experience in particular left its mark on us. It was then when I decided to serve the church through its Christian Social Service programs.

When Mike turned over the keys to me, he wanted to give me his deputy sheriff's badge and showed me his gun, suggesting I should get one of my own. I had never owned a gun. I said to him, "Mike, if it takes a gun to stay here, we probably won't be here too long." I understood that there had been times of crisis at the camp, but I prayed that we could go forward without having to rely on a gun for our safety.

Throughout its history, the camp had been used as a place where others, especially inter-racial groups, brought their programs. As I began my new position, the Aldersgate Advisory Council encouraged me to initiate more programs unique to the camp itself. I felt very strongly that we needed to approach the neighborhood people who lived near the camp, and were among those who did not look favorably on it. I went door-to-door throughout the neighborhood meeting people and suggesting we work together to build programs for their families and children. Most were receptive, and I assured them that Aldersgate wanted to be a good neighbor, but could not accomplish its goals without their support.

With ideas for new programs, I needed volunteers! So, of course, I went to the Methodist churches. Members of area Methodist churches and students in the social work program at Philander Smith College helped with field work by organizing several activities for the neighborhood children. Soon, black and white children were enjoying overnight stays in our cabins and participating in activities together. What a joy!

Space and time do not allow me to share details about all the programs Camp Aldersgate sponsored during my fifteen-plus years there. In almost every one of its programs, enormous progress was made toward better race relations around Little Rock and in Arkansas Methodism. The camp, nearly sixty years old now, has held true to its mission of social justice, racial harmony, and providing life enrichment opportunities in a natural setting. Aldersgate has truly brought PEOPLE together!

Editors' Note:

For more details on Camp Aldersgate, see Nancy Britton's book Camp Aldersgate: A Brief History, *which supplied much of the information for this piece.*

A Minister's Stand
Mabel Harris Webb

"The Light shines in the darkness and the darkness did not comprehend it."
—John 1:5

I humbly share this story as a memorial to my courageous husband, Edward W. Harris, and his long ministry of steadfast commitment to his belief in the Fatherhood of God and the Brotherhood of Man as revealed through the love of Jesus Christ. It is also important that this story be told because of its historical significance in a very troubled time for the country and the Methodist Church.

Edward had a passion for social justice beginning early in his life. His master's thesis revealed that church school education made a difference in young people's attitudes toward race. I felt his 1964 stand, continuing his deep concern for matters of race, was the finest hour of his entire ministry.

The new year of 1964 was dawning. We were in our fourth year at First Methodist Church in Pine Bluff, Arkansas, having moved there in 1960 after nine years of ministry in Louisiana. We discovered the flames of the Civil Rights movement were reaching Pine Bluff, as it was in other communities across the South. A highly publicized Civil Rights activist had come to town to stir up the fires. There were sit-ins at public eating places that where not open to blacks and a real threat of race riots. The tension was growing; white and black people were apprehensive.

Looking back, I recall the events leading up to Race Relations Sunday in February of 1964. Edward and I had attended a gathering in Dallas, Texas, to hear the great missionary from India, Dr. E. Stanley Jones. It was a wonderful spiritual experience. We both were fired up by the Holy Spirit, ready to do whatever the Lord's will was for our lives.

In the following weeks, I was involved with a group of women planning the World Day of Prayer service in February. The theme was "Let Us Pray," the same service used all over the world. Pine Bluff had observed a

World Day of Prayer for twenty-eight years, but for the first time, it was to be inter-racial. This was explosive as the local paper lead with the head-line, "Services to be Open to All Races." Our women's group was committed and had members from Arkansas AM&N, a black college now known as University of Arkansas at Pine Bluff. They were professors' wives at the college and beautiful Christians with whom we had become friends.

One of the World Day of Prayer Services was held in our Wheeler Chapel at noon for accessibility to the business community, as we were a downtown church. At the climax of the Service of Rededication we prayed together: "Lord, let us bind ourselves with willing bonds to you, our Covenant God, taking the yoke of Christ upon us."

In the meantime, Pine Bluff was a boiler of fear, anger, and racial hatred just waiting to explode. Several of our church members had been indignant and critical of their pastor for allowing the service, open to all, in our chapel.

Another annual observance in the Methodist Church is Race Relations Sunday. On this occasion, Ed knew the task before him was to preach the Gospel and take a stand, no matter what. Being a very careful and methodical man, he checked with the bishop of our confer-ence about the sermon he had decided to preach and the stand he was about to take, knowing he was quite possibly going to cause more unrest and dissent. He wanted the bishop's assurance of support in the time to come and received, unequivocally, that assurance.

Emboldened by the Holy Spirit, Edward preached a most eloquent and forceful sermon entitled "A Methodist Pastor and Race Relations." He took his text from Luke 4:18-19: "The Spirit of the Lord is upon me, because He has anointed me to preach good news to the poor; He has sent me to proclaim release to the captives and the recovering of sight to the blind, set at liberty those who are oppressed, to proclaim the acceptable year of the Lord."

Then Ed's sermon began: (these are excerpts)

> My purpose in this message is to interpret to my people the teach-ings and practices of Methodism in the area of race relations and the responsibility that these teachings place upon a Methodist pastor....
>
> There are those who ask the question, "Why does Methodism feel compelled to speak concerning the social needs of people instead of confining its teaching and preaching to the Gospel of personal redemption?" The answer is that Methodism does not consider it to

187

be a question of "either or" but of "both and." We preach both a personal and a social Gospel, and we do not separate them from one another. The Methodist Social Creed from the 1960 *Book of Discipline* contains a statement concerning our Methodist heritage:

> The interest of the Methodist Church in social welfare springs from the Gospel and from the labors of John Wesley, who ministered to the personal, intellectual, and social needs of the people to whom he preached the Gospel of personal redemption. In our historic position we have sought to follow Christ in bringing the whole of life with its activities, possessions, and relationships into conformity with the will of God. As Methodists we have an obligation to affirm our position on social and economic questions.... The Methodist stands for the equal right of all racial, cultural, and religious groups. We confess with deep penitence that our performance as a Church has not kept pace with our profession....'

The Church must work to change those community patterns in which racial segregation appears, including education, housing, voting, employment and the use of public facilities. To insist that restaurants, schools, business establishments, and hotels provide equal accommodations for all people without regard to race or color, but to exempt the Church from the same requirements is to be guilty of absurdity as well as sin. Any Methodist pastor whose hearing is sensitive enough to hear the cries of race and clan that echo now in the streets of our cities knows that the racial tensions accompanying such cries often move into the life of a local congregation.

A pastor is keenly aware of the heavy responsibility that rests upon his shoulders on the point of church membership.... I do not anticipate a rush of applicants for membership when my attitude becomes known to our Negro friends. However, for the large numbers of Negro people who do not apply the knowledge that they are free to choose and are not excluded from a church because of race or color, there will come a new sense of worth to the personalities and a new sense of assurance as professing Christians. For white Christians there will also come a cleansing of conscience and the removal of unspoken and unrecognizable fears that rested heavily on our hearts.

The policy of your pastor is easily understood.... It is found in the printed invitation, which reads, "Those who wish to unite with First Methodist Church will please come forward during the singing of this hymn." As long as I am your pastor, this will continue to be the approach to the matter of church membership, namely, to receive all who are qualified, and who desire to be received without regard to race, color, or national origin.

I hope that you will not mistake my absolute frankness with you this morning for a change in the deep, abiding affection in which I hold for every official and member of First Methodist Church, Pine Bluff, Arkansas.

Whether you agree with my conception of a Methodist pastor's responsibility in the field of race relations or not, I trust that you will remember me as a pastor who always dealt with the theme of race relations in terms of God's Love for every child of His, in terms of a Christ who died for every man, and in terms of the work of the Holy Spirit who is no respecter of persons.

My closing plea is for spiritual unity in the life of the Church. When we ask others whose skins are another color to share a service of worship in our own church, we quickly discover whether the 'Love of Christ constraineth us' or whether we are ruled and directed by our prejudices. When faith demands that we cross that line which separates works and actions, we may truly become 'broken bread' and 'poured out wine' for our Christian convictions and for Christ's sake.

These are days when the divisive faces of prejudice, hatred, greed, selfishness, and secularism threaten the very life of the Christian Church, from the local to the ecumenical level. In the midst of these days, I would counsel church members and officials to remain united at all times in spirit and life. To that end I urge you to study the seventeenth chapter of John's Gospel, which contains the matchless prayer of Jesus for spiritual unity, "that they may all be one as Thou, Father, art in Me, and I in Thee, that they, also, may be one of us."

My prayer for First Church is that Jesus be Lord in all of its Life, and that we may be one in Christ. As your pastor I have spoken without apology in presenting to you what I believe to be the Voice of the Methodist Church and the Voice of my Lord and Savior. I trust my words in your hands, and I surrender them completely into the Hands of God.

The congregation heard his words, knew exactly what he meant and reacted swiftly and furiously. The ushers resigned, fearful and unwilling to face the problem of seating black people who might come on subsequent Sundays. Parishioners who had previously been close friends and generous to us turned quickly against us, and some did not hesitate to say why.

The Board of Stewards met the next week, and the discussion was heated. They declined to support their pastor in his stand, which by then was known to the entire state. They said they did not understand his action; they felt betrayed and asked him repeatedly, "Why did you have to do that?" Only one board member, a prominent doctor, stood up for the preacher, saying he "had never seen any difference between white blood and black blood—it was all red."

The Women's Society of Christian Service was the next to meet. Their disapproval was similarly outspoken. As the pastor's wife, I stood and in our defense quoted some scriptures about love. They fell on deaf ears. The society's president began personally canvassing church members to urge them to withhold their pledges until Annual Conference so that we would not be reappointed.

Despite the bishop's promises of support, and despite the sermon's strong foundation in scripture and published Methodist doctrine, the conference leadership and clergy were silent. The "voice of the Methodist Church" that pervaded the sermon was not heard in its aftermath. Ed felt this to be the worst blow of all—"wounded in the house of his friends."

Although we received so much kindness and love from the members of the congregation the previous three years, it changed overnight. However, there was a very small minority who reached out to us in quiet ways with love and support. A young woman who was searching earnestly for the Lord found a life-changing experience through this turmoil. Teaching a fourth grade Sunday school class, she prayed to find a way to help her pastor and did so. She had the children make little scripture plaques which were painted gold and passed hand to hand through the congregation as Ed preached. The plaques read, "Let us love one another, for love is God." As she grew in love, she reached out to the black community and organized an inter-racial luncheon group called "A Little Bit of Heaven," which met monthly for fellowship and discussion.

As news spread through the community, the White Citizens Council got involved. They were always ready to fan the flames of hostility toward anyone who dared question segregation. The parsonage telephone began to ring off the wall. We could not allow our young daughter to answer it, for so many of the callers threatened our lives. We feared a cross would be burned in our yard. We tried to keep our home life low-key and to keep our spirits up even though we felt the church had deserted us. But we never felt the Lord's presence left us.

Ed continued to preach every Sunday until Annual Conference at the end of May. His sermons were always Christ-centered. I sat in my pew lifting him in prayer, many times wiping away tears. An anthem

190

based on Psalm 27 became "our song," which I played over and over on the piano at home during those months.

The one Christian voice raised publicly in our support was that of a German priest assigned to the local black Catholic Church. He had been sent to Pine Bluff after becoming experienced at handling crisis at other hot spots around the country and was valued as a troubleshooter. The first Sunday after the notorious sermon, he came to First Methodist to hear Ed preach and show his support. Later that afternoon, Ed was completely exhausted and had gone to bed when there was a knock on the door. It was the Father from the Catholic Church. He and I visited for hours. He was compassionate and eager to offer comfort and understanding, and he related our suffering to his own—and the Lord's.

He asked if we knew the meaning of the word "Gethsemane." He demonstrated with his hands: "It is the place of the wine press where they crush the finest of the grapes." He quoted the Lord's words in John 15:20: "A servant is not greater than his master. If they persecute me, they will persecute you" and again from John 13:16 after Jesus had washed his disciples' feet saying, "Truly, truly I say to you, a servant is not greater than his master, nor is he who is sent greater than He who sent him. If you know these things, blessed are you if you do them." What a blessing he was to us! What a great perspective he shared for the experience we were going through. In the weeks that followed, we developed a real friendship together in Christ.

Because of the heated response of our city, and the silence of our Methodist leadership statewide, we expected to be moved out of state when the Annual Conference met in May. Our expectations were realized when Ed received word of an appointment to Ferguson Methodist Church in St. Louis, Missouri, only a week before we were to be there. It was a whirlwind week in which we had to pack and also buy furniture for the unfurnished parsonage we were to occupy. When we arrived at the parsonage door feeling like strangers in a strange land, lo and behold, a gorgeous Peace rosebush was in full bloom by the parsonage door. We understood that as a sign of God's constancy and peace.

Though we had never dreamed we would be back in Arkansas, six years later we were assigned to a church in Little Rock. After serving there a short time, Ed discovered a written policy still on the books in 1970: No Blacks. However, that rule was broken on Boy Scout Sunday.

A black boy had been admitted to the troop by a beloved veteran Scout Master of fifty years whom nobody would question. He had invited the parents of the boys in his troop to the morning worship service. We breathed a sigh of relief when it was over.

Shocked at the continuance of such a policy, Ed left after two years to take a non-pastoral appointment as director of the Christian Civic Foundation of Arkansas. The Civic Foundation was an organization devoted to the Church's stands on alcohol, drugs, gambling, and pornography. It was an unpopular job with a small salary, serving as a lobbyist in the state legislature for the Methodist and Baptist churches. He served in that position with distinction for the last ten years of his ministry, retiring in 1981, but we missed the warm love of a congregation and a parsonage home.

Even after retirement, Ed continued to feel the effects of those painful weeks in Pine Bluff. While he never abandoned his faith or his church, he periodically suffered from bouts of depression, nightmares, and Post Traumatic Stress Disorder. Over forty years after the trauma and only two weeks before his death in 2004, he told Elizabeth, our daughter, that he had just had one of the worst nightmares of his life. He told her, "I was in a race riot. It was ugly, brutal and disturbing, and I was right in the middle of it." He was ninety-three.

In 1979, Philander Smith, a traditionally black college supported by the United Methodist Church, awarded Ed an honorary Doctor of Divinity degree for his long ministry and work with civil rights. Ed was deeply touched and grateful. It was the only public recognition for his stand by any Methodist institution.

The Epworth Leagues
Miller Williams

In 1946, my father was a Methodist minister serving a church in Fort Smith, Arkansas. He and the minister of the local African Methodist Episcopal Church arranged to have young people from their Sunday evening gatherings, called Epworth Leagues, meet together on a regular basis. Some members of our church, of course, dropped out and there were some loud protests, but the two ministers stuck by their decision. Most of the members continued to attend church.

After a few weeks of meeting together, we decided to attend a Fort Smith High School basketball game together. We went on a Saturday afternoon and sat in the white section of the stadium. There were grumblings and threats and people moved away from us, but we held our ground for most of the game. When we did leave the stadium, some white students ran up behind us. I was whirled around and hit in the face with a fist. I lost several teeth that night. My friends helped me home and told my parents what had happened. Both reacted as if I'd earned a Purple Heart.

Editors' Note:

Miller Williams is Professor Emeritus of English at the University of Arkansas in Fayetteville and internationally acclaimed for his books on poetry and literary criticism. In 1997, he was chosen by President William Jefferson Clinton to be his Inaugural Poet.

Racial Unrest and Pastoral Ministry—A Crisis of Conscience
John S. Workman

Imagine three snapshots, fading tintypes that haunt an aging memory:

* Photo One: A Sunday morning, standing in the sanctuary entrance-way, greeting parishioners after the morning service. Familiar faces, smiles, good fellowship among friends whose joys, sorrows, failures and successes have been shared for a half-dozen years.

   A neighbor, grim expression on unsmiling face, is next in line: "Preacher, you said a dirty word in your sermon this morning."

   I knew immediately the "word" he meant: "Martin Luther King, Jr."

* Photo Two: A mid-week morning in the pastor's study, enjoying some too-rare quiet time. Pondering sermon ideas, studying scripture, writing notes. The telephone rings.

   "John, are you sitting down?"

   The caller, a fellow pastor in an east Arkansas community where I was soon to be guest preacher at a weeklong revival meeting: "John, I'm going to have to un-invite you to our church."

   The un-invitation came as no surprise. What had surprised me was that I had been invited in the first place. Word had gotten around that the invited guest preacher was "on that list"—one of those "young Turks" whose liberal views on the currently boiling race issues were unacceptable, would be disturbing, would be unsettling for the church and unwelcome in the community. He was one whose presence would be certain to inflame already simmering racial animosities.

   It would be decades later before I was to put that memory in proper perspective: John, in truth, you may have been given, whether you deserved it or not, a high compliment on your ministry.

* Photo Three, another time, another place: At a dining table in a small restaurant on the north side of Newport. Three of us: the

pastor of a nearby church where I was the week's guest speaker, his wife, and myself.

We had heard the news shortly before we entered the café: Martin Luther King, Jr., had been fatally shot in nearby Memphis. The city was in violent turmoil. We were stunned, and totally unprepared for the scene in the restaurant, where the news had obviously gotten around among the few dozen diners. While some appeared subdued, quiet and troubled, others were in what could only be called a celebratory mood.

During the preceding days, the entire region, as indeed the entire nation, had watched the mounting tension in Memphis as Dr. King continued his crusade in support of the city's striking sanitation workers. Feelings were high. Violence was in the air. And then came the news of the shooting.

Within the hour I would stand in the pulpit to preach.

* * *

The Elephant in the Pastor's Study

Such snapshots are, of course, only one pastor's hazy recollections, brief glimpses of the multitudes of happenings, circumstances and challenges faced daily by many Americans during the 1950s and '60s, those years of racial strife.

While most sensitive citizens struggled with the issues, "the racial crisis" had special import for clergypersons. For those whose duty and privilege it was to stand in the pulpit to preach and give daily pastoral care in times of grief, illness, joy and the host of other life experiences, those years were not only a time of crisis in race relations. They were, for numerous pastors, what could properly be called a time of crisis of conscience.

If the racial crisis was "the elephant in the living room" in many American homes, a huge problem too often ignored, that crisis of conscience was the elephant in the pastor's study. It was, for this pastor at least, the ever-present, ever-gnawing, ever-overwhelming challenge affecting almost every aspect of daily ministry. It was the elephant on the pastor's back.

At least that's the way I felt at the time, and I suspect my experience was not untypical, especially among younger pastors who considered themselves liberals. But, of course, not all pastors felt that way. There were many who saw the separation of the races as the natural order of things, "the way God intended it." For those pastors, the suggestion of a crisis of conscience sounded like nonsense.

Although generalizations are not fair, the conservative group consisted mostly of older ministers who had grown up with the status quo and saw little reason for the church to get overly excited about racial issues. Some of those conservative pastors were outspoken in their position and found support among many laypersons.

But hear a confession from this pastor who was in the liberal camp: In hindsight, the perception of those years as primarily "a crisis," failed to recognize the fundamental nature of the events: That "the crisis" was, in fact, an opportunity. A challenging and difficult opportunity, yes, but nevertheless an opportunity. But more on that later.

Herewith a warning to readers: If what follows is not especially "fun reading," let me assure you it was not fun writing. Much of what follows is in the nature of confession, and it's not much fun to confess. Nor is it in good taste to broadcast one's confessions. And furthermore, nice people shouldn't enjoy listening in as someone else is being wracked by the agonies of confession.

Nevertheless, this writer submits to this unpleasant exercise for two reasons: First, like other contributors to this collection, he was invited to do so (on a topic of his own choosing). And second, these confessions may, with his blessing, shed light on how the tensions of the times affected some pastors.

And, with his second blessing, these confessions might somehow be of help to young pastors who face the overwhelming challenges of ministry in today's difficult and challenging times.

The Nature of the Beast

How to characterize the crisis of conscience felt by many pastors during those years of turmoil? Perhaps a quick look at the nature of the minister's task—his and her calling and role—might provide insight into the dynamics of that crisis, at least from the perspective of this particular pastor.

The challenge: How does a shepherd of a flock handle the often-conflicting tensions inherent in the minister's historic three-fold role: that of being, at one and the same time, a pastor (a comforter); a prophet (a "confronter"); and a priest (a mediator between humans and the Divine, as when administering the sacraments)?

To illustrate: How may a pastor "comfort the afflicted" and, when the prophet role requires, "afflict the comfortable," without at the same time "putting a roadblock" between the parishioner and his or her relationship to the Divine?

How can I speak my conscience and be faithful to my convictions without cutting myself off from the very people to whom I must minister in times of their deepest need?

If one of your loved ones had just died, would you want to be ministered to by a pastor whose views on racial issues enraged you? Could you receive from such a pastor the comfort of which you were so in need? For this pastor, such questions and issues constituted a continual tension, a continuing crisis of conscience.

Challenge and tension are, of course, a part of ministry. They go with the territory, as every pastor knows. They are faced not only in regard to racial issues, but also in numerous other arenas of ministry. I experienced the same crisis of conscience when dealing with theological issues. I often found it difficult to be totally honest as a preacher and pastoral teacher. I soft-peddled many of my liberal views regarding the Bible, such as issues regarding literal interpretations, miracles, and other topics on which parishioners had strongly held opinions and convictions different from my own. Too often I pulled my punches.

I now know that I was wrong in not being more honest. I was wrong not to trust my parishioners more. I should have been more willing to express my own beliefs and my own doubts. I should have shared my belief that our doubts could, in fact, be a way to greater faith; that, as one author has said, "There lives more faith in honest doubt than in half the creeds." But I was afraid that if I were so frankly honest, I might damage the faith of young seekers.

It was, however, in the inflammatory issue of race that I personally felt this crisis of conscience most heavily. In those years "the race question" was truly the explosive issue. The unity of many congregations was threatened. Although I frequently spoke to the issue in my sermons, I never felt particularly successful in doing so. I felt that I didn't faithfully fulfill the prophetic role of ministry. I agonized and struggled with the question, "How can one be a faithful pastor and also, at the same time, a faithful prophet?"

I knew, of course, that it had been and was being done. I knew pastors, and read of others, who were doing it, who could both "comfort and confront." Such ability, however, seemed rare, and I hated that I either didn't have it or was unsuccessful in discovering or developing it.

Crisis or Opportunity?

It was only in retrospect, alas, too late, that I was to realize the true nature and significance of what I have called a crisis in conscience and its import for pastors. Amidst the tensions and turmoil of the time, I failed to recognize a fundamentally important truth: That crisis is just another word for opportunity.

Rather than being a crisis, those years were in fact a time of great opportunity. They offered an invitation to give witness to what I believed. They were a chance to proclaim the gospel of love and the equal worth and value, in the eyes of God, of every human being. Those years were an opportunity to help a struggling community find a better way, to reverse long-standing patterns of injustice, to confess past sins, to heal old animosities, to work for reconciliation among all of God's people.

Once again it grieves me to confess that those days presented a challenge I failed to fully accept, or, perhaps, to fully understand as an opportunity. At the time I felt that I had failed in trying to give my best. I felt I had not said enough. I felt there was always more that I should do. As old sailors would put it, I felt that I'd missed my tide.

I remember agonizing over whether I should travel to Alabama to stand with others in support of Martin Luther King, Jr., to be physically present outside that jail in Birmingham, to give one more body in visible witness. But at the time I was, I suppose, just too afraid to do it.

I considered what it would mean for my wife and our then two children, and how my parishioners would react, how my ministry among them would be affected. And, yes, I suspect I was also afraid of what such a then-radical action would mean for my "career" in the Annual Conference. I didn't make that pilgrimage. I chickened out.

It helped little to remember that none other than the Apostle Paul experienced similar agonies: "I do not understand my own actions. For I do not do what I want, but I do the very thing I hate" (Romans 7:15, RSV). Nor did it help to realize that some people function well when faced with controversy and others do not. Some have the ability to react positively, others respond negatively and defensively. Different folks, different strokes.

In retrospect, I felt that I was not among those who had the gifts and graces to handle such situations of intense face-to-face conflict. That realization was not then, nor is it now, a pleasant thing to acknowledge.

All of this said, however, there was a part of me that was keenly aware of the importance of those moments in history. But this half-century later, it still comes as an embarrassing confession: I felt that in so many ways I was not up to the task. I felt that although I tried to be faithful to my convictions, in effect I had failed. The pain of those feelings haunts me to this day.

One intention of this rather un-savory public display of personal confession is to give insight into what went on in the minds and hearts of many clergypersons during America's racial crisis of the mid-twentieth century. A thin slice of reality; what it was like to minister in the midst of the turmoil, in the eye of the hurricane, in the vortex of the storm. But in truth, authentic prophetic ministry has never been easy. When was it ever otherwise?

But behold a wonder: As the gospel promises, there is always grace, always a second chance. For me, that second chance came in a new type of ministry; religious journalism. Now let the curtain rise on the second act of this confessional drama.

* * *

In Which the Guilty is Given a Second Chance

After twenty years as a pastor, my career took a sudden and unexpected change of course. I was asked to become editor of *The Arkansas Methodist*, the then-weekly newspaper of our denomination's Arkansas area. After a careful weighing of the decision, I accepted.

Aside from being totally overwhelmed with the new challenge (I had never even had a course in journalism), I dug in and worked long and difficult hours to learn what the job was all about. Being immediately faced with reporting on two Annual Conference sessions was a true baptism by fire. Not only was I the reporter (had to get all the facts right!), I was also the photographer, editorial and column writer, the paper's business manager and the area's public information person. During those early weeks I worked into the wee hours, a necessity I soon learned to be part of the territory.

During those years (1973-1979), denominational newspapers were in a transition period. Some that had been traditionally independent, managed by their own boards rather than overseen by a church board, began to surrender some of their independence in order to have greater financial support from church agencies. As a result, those papers slowly became, in effect, "house organs" (as compared with secular newspapers, which traditionally have an "adversary relationship" with society's power structures).

As editor of the *Methodist*, I resisted that trend as long as possible. I was convinced that the church needed a voice that was free of "editorial restraint" from denominational structures. I felt that just as the secular press best served the community by maintaining its adversarial nature, the church was best served by a similarly independent voice.

Hence, in my editorials, if I believed circumstances called for it, I didn't temper the wind to the church's power structures. I sought to fulfill the prophet's admonition to declare, "Thou art the man." Although it was rare that circumstances called for such a critical stance, but when it did, it made for an interesting time.

It wasn't long, however, before economics forced *The Arkansas Methodist* to seek more financial support from the two Conferences. And with that increased support came greater editorial control. True to the pattern elsewhere, the *Methodist*, to my regret, lost some of its independence and, lamentably, joined the growing number of church "house organs." That development was, in my opinion, a significant loss to the church.

To pick up on the narrative regarding my years as a pastor, I found that writing (as compared to preaching) was "more my thing." I felt much freer to speak my conscience and mind on controversial issues.

Part of that freedom, I'm sure, was because I felt somewhat "liberated" from the restraints and tensions that go with being a pastor. As no longer "pastor, prophet and priest," I felt freer to deal more honestly and forthrightly with controversial issues. I know it shouldn't have been that way, many pastors could fulfill all three roles, but in my case, that's the way it was.

That is not to say that I was unconscious of the responsibilities and privileges given to a newspaper editorialist and columnist. Quite the contrary: I was deeply conscious of that responsibility and sought to be true to the trust placed in me. Among the many controversial issues I addressed in my columns and editorials (at both the Methodist and later at the Arkansas Gazette) were those regarding race. A newspaper column provided me an opportunity to say things I'd failed to say, or was perhaps too "timid" to say, as a pastor. Since my years at the Methodist came long after the scope of this volume's focus (the racial strife of the '50s and '60s), it seems inappropriate to dwell further on my time there.

Mr. Writer Goes to Third and Louisiana

After being at the Methodist for six years, I spoke to the bishop about the possibility of my approaching the Arkansas Gazette on becoming their full-time religion editor. He gave his permission. I popped the question, and the Gazette hired me—with the stipulation that I would come as a totally objective writer, with no bias or favor shown toward my own denomination.

I'd long had great respect for the Arkansas Gazette. I admired its editorial positions and its newspaper-of-record reputation as the oldest newspaper west of the Mississippi River. Its Pulitzer Prize for news coverage and editorial writing during the Central High School racial crisis was, to me, not only a confirmation of those opinions, but was a shining example of the importance of a free and courageous press.

I had long felt that some of the best preaching I'd ever heard, I'd read on the editorial and opinion pages of secular newspapers. Some of those writings made me think that if the Apostle Paul had it to do over again, he would have been a journalist.

I was proud to be a member of the Gazette staff. I seldom entered that building at Little Rock's Third and Louisiana streets without feeling a sense of awe, if I might use that word. I was humbled to be among what I considered some of the best writers of the time. In my column writing, I felt a heavy responsibility to speak a meaningful and helpful word to some of the most significant issues facing our state and nation. It was an honor to have such a privilege.

Controversy? Yes, indeed. Almost weekly, if not daily. Many of the liberal opinions I expressed in my weekly columns were offensive to some readers and evoked heated responses in the paper's Letters to the Editor. Some of those letters hit hard, but that was part of the territory. They expressed the deeply held opinions of readers. All of that exchange, my opinions and those of readers, contributed to the public debate, which I felt was an important exercise in democracy. I felt honored by the privilege and responsibility entrusted to me as a columnist in what had long been the state's leading newspaper.

In Retrospect

From the tenor of much of Act I (my years as a pastor) in this two-part drama, it would be easy to conclude that the crisis of conscience associated with the race issues of the 1950s and '60s meant that my years as a pastor were unhappy. Quite the contrary is true.

Although I certainly agonized over the race issue, and other controversial issues as noted, I still had many gratifying and happy times in the pastorate. The satisfactions and rewards of pastoral ministry, and the many lasting friendships made, are a grand treasure for me and for our family.

And, all things considered, I must have done some things right as a pastor in regard to the racial strife issues. I participated in numerous events and activities to promote racial harmony; I joined with colleagues in efforts to encourage the integration of Hendrix College; and I tried, as a pastor, to help my congregations become a part of the solution to the many-faceted race problems.

And I suppose I rightly earned the reputation of being "one of those young pastors" who had the impertinence to afflict the comfortable. Years later I allowed myself to accept that reputation, and view events such as my being "un-invited" to preach that revival meeting, as badges of honor (again, whether I truly deserved them or not).

Regarding the pastoral ministry, I still believe it is the single most important calling to which a young man or woman, and older ones, too, could devote their lives. I don't know of a more significant task. Nor do I know of one that, when faithfully fulfilled, is more difficult.

Editors' Note:

This map demonstrates the active hate groups in Arkansas. It is taken from www.tolerance.org, a website of the Southern Poverty Law Center that seeks to create a national community committed to human rights. Its goal is to awaken people of all ages to the problems of hate and intolerance, to equip them with the best tolerance ideas, and to prompt them to take right action in their homes, schools, businesses and communities.

All is not yet well.

9 780970 857446